THE
ghost town
STORYTELLER

THE
ghost town
STORYTELLER

NAOMI BLACK

Principal photographer Jack Deutsch

MALLARD
PRESS

A FRIEDMAN GROUP BOOK

Published by MALLARD PRESS
An Imprint of BDD Promotional Book Company, Inc.
666 Fifth Avenue
New York, N.Y. 10103

Mallard Press and the accompanying duck logo are
registered trademarks of BDD Promotional Book Co., Inc.
Registered in the U.S. Patent and Trademark Office.

Copyright © 1992 by Michael Friedman Publishing Group, Inc.

First published in the United States of America in 1992 by
The Mallard Press

ISBN 0-7924-5770-6

THE GHOST TOWN STORYTELLER
was prepared and produced by
Michael Friedman Publishing Group, Inc.
15 West 26th Street
New York, New York 10010

Editors: Stephen Williams and Kelly Matthews
Art Director: Jeff Batzli
Designer: Kingsley Parker
Photography Editor: Ede Rothaus

Typeset by Trufont
Color separations by United South Sea Graphic Art Co.
Printed and bound in Hong Kong by Leefung-Asco
Printers Ltd.

Grateful acknowledgement is given to authors, publishers,
and photographers for permission to reprint material. Every
effort has been made to determine copyright owners of photographs and illustrations. In the case of any omissions, the
Publishers will be pleased to make suitable acknowledge-
ments in future editions.

Principal Photographer: Jack Deutsch

Photographs by Jack Deutsch pp.: Front jacket, back jacket,
2, 3, 8, 10, 12, 13, 15, 16, 17, 18, 19, 21, 23, 24, 25, 26, 28, 30,
31, 32, 33, 34, 35, 36-37, 40, 42, 43, 44, 45, 46, 47, 48, 49,
51, 52-53, 58, 60, 62, 64, 65, 66, 67, 68, 69, 71, 72, 73, 74,
75, 76, 79, 80, 81, 82, 83, 85, 86, 88, 89, 90, 93, 94, 95

With other contributions from:

Alaska State Library pp. 102, 104, 106, 107, 108, 109 (upper
right), 110, 113, 114, 117, end papers
Colorado Historical Society pp. 58, 63, 68, 74
Alissa Crandall pp. 102, 109
Courtesy Death Valley National Monument pp. 28, 30, 34, 39
Ken Graham pp. 105
Ken Graham Agency pp. 102, 109 (lower right), 111, 112, 115, 116
Montana Historical Society, Helena, MT pp. 90, 96, 97, 99, 100
Courtesy Museum of New Mexico pp. 2, 57; photographs by
Henry A. Schmidt pp. 40, 47, 48, 50, photography by
W. Edmunds Claussen pp. 55
Nevada Historical Society pp. 20, 27
Ede Rothaus pp. 55, 56
Wyoming State Museum pp. 79, 84, 85, 86

Acknowledgments

A thank you to last as long as the spirit of a ghost town goes to Jean Mills whose research on the Rocky Mountain states provided me with a solid base from which to work.

Thanks, too, to Stephen Williams, my first editor on this book. He asked me one too many times, and I said yes. It's always a pleasure working with Stephen.

I'd like to also acknowledge Kelly Matthews, who arrived when Stephen left and whose good nature and sharp eyes have helped considerably; Ede Rothaus, the photo editor; and Jack Deutsch. With Jack's dedication to speed and quality, this book is immeasurably improved.

Many thanks should also go to all the people we met in the ghost towns and to all the librarians, historians, and ghost town watchers who contributed the tales, tips, and truths that have enriched the book.

For John
Susannah and Tobiah

Contents

Colorado

Wyoming

Montana

Klondike

Introduction

On December 6, 1848, the headline of Washington's *Daily National Intelligencer* read PRESIDENT'S ANNUAL MESSAGE. The article began:

It was known that mines of precious metals existed to a considerable extent in California at the time of its acquisition. Recent discoveries render it probable that these mines are more extensive and valuable than was anticipated. The accounts of the abundance of gold in that Territory are of such an extraordinary character as one would scarcely command belief.

President James Polk's words to the American public flashed across the country from the East to the West Coasts, igniting a fever in hundreds of thousands of people. Not everyone left for the goldfields, but at the very least, they probably considered it. People's imaginations had been sparked. There was romance to the idea of a regular Joe or Jane working a plot of land and finding a fortune. It was the American dream—and it wasn't confined to California.

The Hearst fortune started in the western mines; John Studebaker of car fame earned his nest egg there; Mack of Mack trucks acquired his capital a little later in the Klondike rush, as did Sid Grauman and Alex Pantages who later became prominent in the movie industry. With-

out the gold rush, Cole Porter might not have had the opportunity to become one of the greatest American songwriters; his father was a forty-niner. Many more men of recognizable fame have the gold rush to thank for their family fortunes. Although few people actually became millionaires from the mines, many earned huge sums by selling goods or services in the camps. It was indeed the American dream.

And the dream continues. Even today, prospectors comb the hills for that one lost mine undetected by the sophisticated machines that dominate the geological trades. One independent miner in Nevada takes in seventy-five thousand dollars a month, but he still prefers his trailer home to the showcase he built nearby. His is a true prospector's heart.

In this book, we set out to find that heart of gold, the human side of the western boom. Towns that died or fizzled to only a ghost of their former glory were so alive during their heydays. The people who found their way to these often isolated sites dealt with tragedy and prosperity on a scale that can be hard to imagine. At the other extreme was the boredom of tedious daily routines that often wrought nothing more than aches and pains. We've endeavored to tell these stories simply and plainly, for it is the people behind the stories and the towns behind the people that deserve to be heard.

Only historians know for sure what the facts are, and even then, truth often blends too closely with fiction. We are enthusiasts, not historians. We've attempted to bring a true picture to life whether through a tall tale or a story of a historic event. There are wonderful books of history out there—in libraries, bookstores, and historical societies—that go into great and often exciting detail. They are well worth delving into. We've barely scratched the surface in bringing these stories together. Read on. We are indebted to all of the authors—amateur historians, academics, and ghost-town buffs—who gathered information from primary and secondary sources that would have been out of our reach if not for them.

Through these sources we hope to bring you a sense of life in the booming towns that grew from small gold camps (silver and other ores—even water—also fueled these towns). Overall, the times were hard. Panning gold (also called "placering") was a painstaking process of monotonously swirling water in a pan until the heavier gold flakes fell to the pan bottom while the lighter sand got flicked out. The coordination of hand and eye and water was an art. Without an expert's touch, the gold could easily go sailing out of the pan with the sandy water. And only an expert's eye could differentiate fool's gold, pyrite, from the real thing. With so much at stake, men strove to become "experts" quickly.

As they learned their craft, most of the prospectors lived in substandard conditions. Canvas and frame shelters shot up while entrepreneurs rented out cots for eight-hour shifts twenty-four hours a day. Baths were a luxury, as was any food besides flour, beans, and salt pork. Most miners longed for home. The western adventure was a temporary evil in their minds, especially for those who made no money.

Once ore was found in an area, businessmen moved in to buy out claims. They put up stamp mills and other buildings that processed the ore and then hired the poorest men whose money was spent. These miners toiled in superheated 100°F (38°C)-plus conditions underground. Aboveground, their wealthy employers often built mansions. But if the ore gave out and there was no other industry to replace mining, everyone lost. The towns died, some more slowly than others.

Despite these hardships and the possibility of despair and failure, the tantalizing legends of the West are still strong. Ironically, it is stories like the ones included here that are bringing new life to some of the West's ghost towns. As city-dwellers are leaving their urban environments for quieter locales, they're stumbling onto the historic ruins of the mining booms—and they're reveling in the stories associated with them. With patience and care, the residents of many of these towns are restoring them. And like the phoenix, many towns will rise again.

1.

Eldorado Canyon

I have deserted Fort Mohave and fixed my quarters at the silver mines. Silver has already been obtained from ten or twelve leads. . . . A capitalist from San Francisco [George Hearst] has been here and purchased stock and we expect brisk times here as soon as steamboats can reach here from San Francisco.

—letter from James M. Sanford to friend
John Brown, December 20, 1862

When they thought of Eldorado, few miners thought of "the gilded one," the tribal leader who dusted himself with gold. They knew, instead, the legend of the land, a mythical city whose streets were paved with gold and where precious gems tumbled about like loose, dry weeds. Plenty for the picking, if only you could find it. No wonder an adventurer might choose Eldorado as a town name. And not just in Nevada. In boomtown days, fourteen states claimed their own Eldorado.

Captain George Johnson named the area although he was not the first to pass through. During his exploration of the lower Colorado River by steamboat in 1857–58, he supposedly wrote:

In February 1869, the Virginia and Truckee Railroad pushed through from Gold Hill (opposite, inset) to Carson City. Trains often made the difference between life and death in a waning gold camp.

*U*ntouched by the flood that swept away the small community of Nelson's Landing near Eldorado in 1974, this old car (above) has been preserved by the sands.

We arrived at the mouth of a canyon which I judge to be the farthest point to which navigation can be carried. I named the canyon El Dorado.

Historians argue over which non-Indian party first noted the canyon and its environs. Geological surveyors in the early 1850s met prospectors when they arrived, so they were not the first. Perhaps it was the ancestors of "a group of better class Mexicans" who rode up to the Wall Street Mine in 1882 and asked a fellow named John Powers if he owned the mine. When he answered yes, they rode away, but not before telling him of a map they had. Drawn by Spanish padres, it was said, the map was very old and apparently very correct, because the Mexicans had ridden directly to the mine.

Some forty miles (64.3 km) south of Las Vegas, the town site of Eldorado Canyon—once the busiest river port in Nevada—now lies beneath the waters of Lake Mohave. Where steam-driven paddleboats once plied, delivering goods for miners and returning to San Francisco with gold, motorboats now provide thrills for today's pleasure seekers. In steamboat days, boating was far from being a leisure-time activity. Muddy water and shifting sandbars were constantly troubling the skippers, who solved the problem by backing into the sandbars until the revolving paddles had rearranged the sand to allow for safe passage.

When accounts of a rich lode of silver or gold in Eldorado Canyon first came in, no one

believed it. They thought it was just one more scheme to unload relatively worthless stock. Once Joseph Good found the Techatticup Mine in 1861, however, people began arriving. By 1863, a garrison of soldiers was sorely needed. The nearest sheriff's office was no less than two hundred miles (321 km) away, through arid, rough country. Like many "lawless" towns of its day, the Eldorado camp made its own law, which often protected absentee owners.

By the early 1870s, a man named John Nash had put together a business called the Eldorado Company and proceeded to take over the Techatticup Mine. With his control came strange rumors of men disappearing when wages were owed them, of workers fearing their boss and not saying why, and of slippery deals involving the Old West equivalent of rubber checks. So it came as no surprise to some when Nash decided to jump an absentee owner's claim—specifically George Hearst's Queen City claim.

Isolated Eldorado attracted killers, thieves, and other gunslingers whose reputations preceded them, so Nash had no trouble finding men to accept a claim-jumping assignment. Jim Jones was one of these men. Known around town as a half-breed horse thief, he'd escaped the law by running to Eldorado. William Piette, whose desire to be a criminal outweighed his actual acts, was another. Last was J. Harrington, a man with three deaths to his name. Not long after Nash hired the trio, Hearst's agent turned up dead; not surprisingly, he had missed the refiling deadline necessary to keep the Queen City claim active.

Some say that Nash never intended any of his lackeys to live, that he secretly hired Piette to kill Harrington and Jones, planning to then take care of Piette himself. In the end, however, Piette needed very little convincing to make Jones his mark, because when the time came for payment, Jones made an error that sealed his fate. Jones refused Nash's note for the agreed-upon five hundred dollars; he wanted cash, a sure sign of distrust.

Outside of Jones' cabin stood a halved powder keg—a "keeler"—that he used as a sink. Piette never gave him a chance. He shot Jones from behind, but only wounded him. Jones countered and tripped his killer. The next events are as muddy as the water that ran from Jones' knocked-over keeler. The action was fast and fanciful. Either Jones grabbed Piette's gun or he ran for his own with Piette in close pursuit. Whichever happened, one more shot rang out, and this time Piette was down. Whether Piette was wounded, turned tail and ran, or was shot dead varies from story to story. In any case, the town was roused.

Their prejudices inflamed by a "half-breed" killer, the mob caught up with Jones quickly. The dry heat slowed the wounded man, who needed water. He ran on fear alone. His tracks, bloodied and uncovered, led his pursuers on a straight path, but Jones did not give up the fight. When confronted, he popped off one shot, dropping the leader of the mob, Tom King.

Jones grabbed King's gun and ran again. But he was tiring.

He ducked into an old prospector's hole, deep enough to give him cover, shallow enough to allow him to shoot. Perhaps he planned to

hold them off until nightfall and then make a run for it, but he never got the chance. The posse found him and closed in, staying just out of range. One day passed with no hope of escape. A second day passed and Jones was barely alive. It took all of his energy just to fire the gun and fend off his assailants. His thirst

Said to be cursed, the town of Eldorado now lies buried under the waters of Lake Mohave (above), a man-made reservoir. A handful of gamblers maintain mining claims in the canyon, but most mine sites are not active.

and the wound, now infected, were enemies attacking him at even closer quarters. There was nothing left to do but surrender. Ripping off a scrap from his sweat- and blood-soaked shirt, he fashioned a flag and raised his gun barrel in capitulation.

With King dead, a man named Tom Johnson took the lead and approached Jones' hole with a pistol in his hand. The sight of the broken man sickened Johnson but compassion had nothing to do with vigilante law. So when Jones pleaded for a drink, Johnson gave him a quick bullet to the head instead. The single shot brought the others, who took turns pumping more lead into the dead body. His burial was nothing more than sand kicked into the hole.

Typical of western tales, the action may have ended but the story continues. Piette's and Harrington's versions of the initial attack varied widely, and the town became a little less sure they'd shot the right man. After killing Jones, Johnson's conscience haunted him until he died, which was not long after. Another vigilante, a supposed upholder of justice, got caught stealing horses and was shot. Piette killed a few more men, then ran for the Mexican border. And Nash, with stories of Jones' ghost haunting the mine, became so uncomfortable that he avoided the Queen City claim altogether. Workers became increasingly skittish, and Nash finally closed the plagued mine.

Jones' ghost continued to make trouble. For decades afterward, mysterious deaths were attributed to his revenge.

Then, in 1897, Eldorado faced another gruesome incident. The story begins with a simple injustice, at least a perceived injustice. Very few women lived or passed through Eldorado Canyon, so when Avote, a Paiute Indian, thought that Lars Frandsen had eyes for his lovely wife, Avote went berserk. He hid behind a rock waiting for Frandsen to pass and shot both Frandsen and his partner as they stopped to water their teams, which were laden with ore from the mill at Eldorado. Leaving his enemy dead, Avote ran, killing all white settlers who crossed his path, even if they had no knowledge of his crime. If he wiped out the intruders, Avote believed, the canyon would once again belong to his people.

What motivated him? No one knows for sure, yet one old-timer tells a similar story of an Indian named Abood who killed Frandsen and who had a definite motive for the killing. (Most likely, Avote and Abood were the same person.) According to Paiute tradition, if one member of the tribe has wronged another, the closest family member must punish the wrongdoer. In this case, Abood's brother slew a mail carrier for gambling money. Abood then had to kill his brother; the deed drove him crazy and that's when he caught up with Frandsen. The settlers knew better than to follow the Indian into his own territory. Instead, they told his tribe of his offense. Either they or neighboring Indians ended the saga of Abood by bringing his head in as proof of his demise. And, some people say, as proof of the curse on Eldorado.

Bullfrog and Rhyolite

Rhyolite, Rhyolite, land of the golden dust!
Rhyolite, Rhyolite, we're going there or bust;
Rhyolite, Rhyolite, just wait till we get back
From Rhyolite, Rhyolite, with nuggets in our sack.
                    —to the tune of "Wyoming"

Bullfrog, Nevada, edges up to Death Valley, its town site not quite within the northeastern boundaries of the Death Valley National Monument, which marks the lowest point of elevation in the United States. The funny-sounding town sprang up in 1904 after an earnest, roving prospector named Frank "Shorty" Harris—aka the "Death Valley Terrapin"—finally discovered a paying claim of greenish-hued ore. He'd been looking for twenty-six years. Shorty shared his discovery with Ernest "Ed" Cross, although Ed said it was the other way around. They high-tailed it to Goldfield to assay the ore and celebrate.

Not a keen businessman, Shorty had a little too much "Oh Be Joyful"—the miners' favorite whiskey—and sold off his long-sought-after claim for one thousand dollars. A more cautious Cross held onto his half of the claim and later sold it for as much as sixty thousand dollars some say; others believe it was one hundred and twenty-five thousand dollars.

Cross can take credit for naming Bullfrog— at least in one story. Sounds like a joke read the headline in a local paper, but Cross wasn't kidding (or was he?) when he said, "I used to sing or try to sing, 'The bulldog on the bank and the bullfrog in the pool,' and I think that explains why I named my first claim in this section the Bullfrog. . . . I determined to call my first location by that name."

The small camp of Bullfrog gave way to Rhyolite rather unusually. Bullfrog didn't gradually spread into Rhyolite. Nor did Rhyolite eclipse the town of canvas tents and canvas-topped wooden shacks. What happened, wrote old-time journalist C. B. Glasscock, was that "the town of Bullfrog literally took up its bed and walked next door to Rhyolite."

One day in February 1905, the promoters of Rhyolite, who had already laid out the streets, rounded up all the residents of the

Rhyolite's John S. Cook Bank (below) came with a $90,000 price tag, but that still did not ensure the bank's success; it folded within a year of its opening in 1907.

night, after being away a week, he came in staggering weak from the loss of blood, with a deep gash in his head and with the wild look of a maniac. In his disheveled hair, mingled with dirt and blood, were flakes of gold. Zeke is still out of his head, and the boys haven't been able to get a line on the location of the find, but they think it is the lost mine, sure, this time, as all Zeke can say to Mr. FitzFogle, proprietor of the Thirst Dispensary, is "Dry Fogle, Dry Fogle."

So begins a piece in the *Rhyolite Herald* (June 30, 1905) under a column entitled "Death Valley Items." Goes to show you couldn't believe everything you read. Mark Twain and Dan de Quille, among others, built reputations for themselves on tall tales as well as true; journalistic shenanigans thrived in Nevada's and California's boomtowns.

Yet this article aside, many people believed in the tale of the Lost Breyfogle Mine. Now as one story goes—and, as always, there are many—Ohioan Charles Breyfogle made his way to California at the time of the Gold Rush and settled into a cushy job as an elected official in Oakland when news of the Comstock Lode tempted him into the little-known land of Nevada near Austin. He didn't head for the Comstock though; instead, he went toward Death Valley, some say following a lead from forty-niners who had had to abandon their prospecting when their resources ran out.

Breyfogle made sure he had provisions and a mule before he struck out for the area east of the Funeral Mountains where Ash Meadows, a

As he watched the bank being built, a Death Valley character named Panamint Joe foresaw the future when he reportedly said, "Someday white man gone—Indian sleep here." The region was home to Shoshone, Southern Paiute, and Kawaiisu Indians before white settlers displaced them.

tent camps—Bullfrog was one of many—and promised them free lots. They moved as one, and Rhyolite was born in a day. The town took advantage of the nearby springs and set up an ice plant almost immediately. More than one storyteller wrote that just as many prospectors came for the ice-cold beer as for the gold. By 1906, four thousand people called Rhyolite home. The third largest city in Nevada, it boasted indoor plumbing, telephone lines, electricity, railroads, a stock exchange, the first Western bank with a burglarproof time-lock vault, and an opera house. Rhyolite's vivacity perpetuated many stories, including the one about Charles Breyfogle.

Single Blanket Zeke, or the Death Valley sleuth, has discovered the lost Breyfogle mine but is unable to take his friends to the spot. The other

Rhyolite had its own stock exchange, built to handle the many stock certificates—legal and illegal—that came out of the Bullfrog mining district. In only two weeks, the exchange handled more than three quarters of a million transactions for the approximately one hundred and fifty area companies listed. Only one mine, however, the Montgomery Shoshone, delivered steady supplies of ore, but it, like its neighbors, never generated money for the majority of its stockholders.

small watering hole, was located. Once there, he met up with some other prospectors, but in a short time, the entire party fell prey to a party of Paiutes. Breyfogle alone survived the attack. And stranded he was, in the desolation of Death Valley without food, water, shelter, or transportation.

He pushed on and managed to find a low-lipped depression of brackish water he christened Coyote Holes. After that first day, he traveled by the light of dawn. But time beats down on Death Valley wayfarers, and by the second day, the heat began to take its toll. Keeping as much to the northeast as possible, he wandered on, his mind clouding from dehydration. When he saw a strip of green in the distance, he recognized it for what he thought it was: an oasis. However, the man, stripped of his dignity and continuing on with whatever strength he had left, came upon not an oasis but a few scrubs of misleading, dry mesquite.

He persevered. Somewhere on his way either to or from the mesquite patch, Breyfogle stumbled on a piece of quartz practically studded with gold. His prospecting instincts hadn't failed him. Unfortunately, he barely knew where he was. Looking around, he noted red earth and a rock outcrop. He pushed on. The heat forced him to travel at night now, and miraculously, he made his way over approximately two hundred miles of backcountry, across the future town sites of Tonopah and Goldfield, to a spot some forty miles (64.3 km) from Austin, where a rancher luckily found him.

In Austin, the resolute prospector regained his health. He also sent his quartz nugget and others he had collected to assayer Jacob Gooding. Gooding estimated the ore at one hundred thousand dollars per ton. Now most western newspapers at the turn of the century would have had a field day with the news of a prospector like Breyfogle landing in their town, but the *Reese River Reveille* published nary a word on the subject. Whether the silence stemmed from the editor's hope of personal gain or from his unwillingness to see his town fold under the prospect of a newer and richer mine, we will never know. Breyfogle entrusted his information only to the few men he planned to take back in the valley with him. They waited impatiently while Breyfogle got better.

In the autumn of 1864, Breyfogle and his party left town quietly, only to be stopped at the valley by warring Paiutes. They didn't set off again until the next spring. Luck followed them to the Coyote Holes. Breyfogle knew he could find the outcrop from there; he had only to retrace his steps, but finding the mesquite belt proved harder than he expected. The mesquite paled without its leaves in these early months of the year, and the reddish soil led only to one dead end after another. Days passed into weeks before Breyfogle's partners advised him to leave, but he felt so close to discovery that he stayed on.

The next they heard of the unlucky man was in an item in the *Reveille* that had been picked up from the Salt Lake *Telegraph*:

In the late 1980s, the mission-style Las Vegas and Tonopah Railroad depot (below) and a railway car across the street still boasted inhabitants. An active mine now threatens the bank (left) and the rest of the town.

Miss Velma Likens and Miss Gertrude Gensler gave a very enjoyable birthday party Wednesday evening to a few "young" friends at their home on Smith Street. Owing to the scarcity of ladies, several of the best-looking (?) boys in town were togged in skirts, shirt waists, paint, powder, and smiles, and acted the part in the most captivating manner. Games were played upon the "lawn," and the party later repaired to the hospital pavilion where a short hop was enjoyed. A fine lunch was served. The young ladies proved themselves charming hostesses.

—from the *Rhyolite Herald,* July 21, 1905

A *prospector not an investor, Shorty Harris (below) found a number of ore-laden sites, but none as big as Bullfrog. Unfortunately, he couldn't hold his ore any more than he could hold his liquor. In a celebratory stupor, he sold his stake of the Bullfrog claim, which at its highest yielded $3,000 a ton, for $1,000.*

Mr. Granger (a prospector) tells us that Mr. Breyfogle, of Reese River, who is no doubt also reported dead, is traveling by (wagon) train to Salt Lake. . . . Mr. Granger found Mr. Breyfogle at Las Vegas Springs, with two shots in his body and half scalped.

Was Breyfogle stopped? He continued his search for the ore-laden rock until he died. He never found a clue.

But there's another, slightly different Breyfogle tale, with a slightly different ending. He was a quiet man, according to some, a rover with a prospector's heart. To others, he was a peevish, taciturn ex–New Yorker, stout and with thinning hair. And it may have been more than news of the Comstock that motivated Breyfogle to leave his job as county treasurer in California; after close scrutiny, the county coffers came up over eight thousand dollars short. Breyfogle then turned up as a blacksmith in one story and, in another, as a mill hand in the Reese River area.

The Paiutes who threatened his life the first time out play a different role in this second version of the story. No one came after Breyfogle. He went out on his own, found the quartz, then became lost on his way back to camp. Thirsty and aching with hunger, Breyfogle reached his partners with news of his find but supplies were low and the Indians had taken most of their animals. They returned without prospecting further.

The $100,000-per-ton ore shows up as $4,500, enough for the *Reveille* editor to

grubstake Breyfogle for his next try. The story runs much the same from there, but years after the incident, a Paiute man named Ash Meadows Charlie admitted that he had had a hand in Breyfogle's scalping. Truth is certainly stranger than fiction in this Death Valley tale. Charlie said that one young Indian fancied Breyfogle's shoes. For those shoes, Breyfogle got conked on his sunburned, balding head, not scalped. In fact, the Paiutes took the poor man to Las Vegas Springs where he'd be sure to be picked up. An adequate explanation for the two gunshot wounds was never found, but then again neither was Breyfogle's lost mine.

Or was it? To this day, some people claim that Breyfogle's mine turned out to be any number of mines in the vicinity. But there are still a few *breyfoglers*—yes, it became a word, at least in Nevada—out there, looking for lost mines.

Unfortunately, anyone searching for Breyfogle's lode now might have trouble; one historian places the mine on land that lies within a weapons-testing range.

It's not inappropriate that parts of Nevada would end up as weapons-testing sites. Plenty of weapons were tested there at the turn of the century as well.

DUEL TO THE DEATH read one headline in 1905. The shooting took place at 10:30 in the presence of thirty men. In all, eight shots were fired. When it was over, two men lay dead: John Sullivan and James C. Clayton. They were neither outlaws nor evil men; they were simply typical inhabitants of a growing mining town.

Apparently there had been bad feelings between the two men for a couple of days, but no one knows why they faced each other off. No one even came forward to say who fired the first shot. The second shot, however, came from in back of the bar—Sullivan's side of the affair. Clayton stood in front.

This was Rhyolite's first public gun quarrel, and its newsworthiness at the time came from the novelty of the incident. Today, the newspaper coverage is as interesting as the fight. Many newspapers then were not as concerned with the whys and wherefores as they were with the action:

After the first shots, before either man was hit, Sullivan rushed from out of the office, which is at the end of the bar, and the two men came together in the center of the room, both firing at the same time. They fired at very close range, the gun barrels almost touching the bodies.

Sullivan turned twice in his tracks and fell, Clayton adding two shots after falling to the floor. Sullivan rallied and tried to choke Clayton and then gave up the fight. In a few moments, Clayton was dead, and Sullivan died a half hour later.

Fifty thousand glass liquor bottles make up the town's most famous architectural oddity, the 1906 Bottle House, which, though restored in 1925, has suffered some damage recently.

Doctors came too late to help either man. Mrs. Sullivan arrived but to no avail. Although her husband dropped in and out of consciousness, he was too far gone to speak to her.

The duel took place in December. Barely five years later, almost as suddenly as it had grown, Rhyolite's population declined to seven hundred people. In 1911, the train tracks were torn up. Today, the population varies from anywhere around zero to a handful. Tourists spill over from Death Valley National Monument to see what's left of the town and the famous Bottle House, a monument to an anonymous bartender who constructed the place with a combination of newspaper, plaster, and over fifty thousand beer and liquor bottles.

Gold Hill and Virginia City

I can recall when an ornery stranger reeled into a C Street saloon, and pounding on the bar with his six-shooter until the glasses danced, announced: "I'm a roarin' ripsnorter from a hoorah camp, an' I can't be stepped on. I'm an angel from Paradise Valley and when I flap my wings there's a tornado loose. I'm a tough customer to clean up after. Give me some of your meanest whiskey, a whole lot of it, that tastes like bumblebee stings pickled in vitriol. I swallered a cyclone for breakfast, a powder mill for lunch, and haven't begin to cough yet. Don't crowd me."
—Wells Drury, editor of the *Comstock Lode*

Now Virginia City wasn't always called Virginia City nor was it named directly after the eastern state. For in the first rush of prospectors, there was a man, "Old Virginia" Finney, who, according to historian Don Ashbaugh, liked his whiskey. At that time, any prospector worth his gold dust had to be able to walk forty rods without stumbling after drinking his "forty-rod" whiskey. So one night Old Virginia sipped a little too much. The bottle slipped from his hands, and he said, "I baptize ye Virginny Town." So the story goes.

Located roughly between Carson City and Reno in the northwestern corner of Nevada, Gold Hill and then Virginia City sprang up when the placer miners, panning and rocking for gold, kept washing up a thick, blue-gray substance that "Old Frank," a local Mexican man (or maybe it was a Brazilian miner) identified as *mucha plata*. Unfortunately, no one among these early residents spoke Spanish (or Portuguese). They just considered the stuff a pain; it was mucking up their work.

Then Pennsylvanians Ethan Allen Grosch and Hosea Ballau Grosch arrived at the rough camp toting books on metallurgy and mining along with their other possessions. They identified the waste that the others were ignoring and laid claim to a lode on Sun Mountain, which proved to have silver ore valued at thirty-five hundred dollars per ton.

Luck turned on the brothers when Hosea struck his foot with a pick. The wound got worse, surrendering him to blood poisoning before anyone could amputate. Ethan arranged for one of the drifters hanging around the camp to house sit and make sure that no one jumped his claim while he traveled back over the Sierras to settle his and his brother's affairs. Ethan barely had time to mourn his sibling. The young man died, trapped by an area storm, just over two months after his brother.

What happened to the drifter Ethan had let into his home? Henry "Pancake" Comstock took over the brothers' claims and called them his own. He made potholes all over the mountainside in his attempts to locate the accessible ore. Comstock's Lode became known but not immediately famous—not until a while later when another prospector discovered a similarly rich lode on the other side of the mountain.

Now a restored tourist town, Virginia City in its heyday attracted a relatively sophisticated populace. The town's inhabitants included writer Samuel Clemens, who wrote for the Territorial Enterprise in the early 1860s before he gained fame as Mark Twain, and Thomas Maguire, who built the town's first legitimate theater, where private boxes cost ten dollars a show. Maguire's theater went bust, but the newspaper reestablished itself in the 1950s. The newspaper building survived two devastating fires as did the Mackay house (above) and the Fourth Ward school (left), which is now a museum.

Thus began the Washoe Rush, which tantalized and teased many prospectors into making the trip from California to Nevada. Population estimates went from zero in 1850 to almost forty-three thousand in the next ten years, with fifteen thousand people attributed to Virginia City alone.

With the newcomers came offers to buy the original claims. Comstock sold out for "ten dollars in cash and $10,990 in promissory notes," wrote historian Don Ashbaugh. Eilley Orrum held onto her claim, which, with her husband's, paid out fifty thousand dollars a month (others say it was almost a million a year).

Called "Queen of the Washoe," Eilley Orrum was born in Scotland in 1816. She fostered the idea that she could see into the future, and for herself she predicted riches and royalty. But at fifteen, before she met her great wealth, she became a Mormon and traveled to Illinois to marry an elder in the church. An elder he was, too, nearly forty-five years her senior. If that wasn't difficult enough, her husband took her to Salt Lake where he married additional wives. She divorced him only to marry another Mormon who took her further west, into mining country that would one day be famous.

Eilley divorced again, and even though her husband returned to Salt Lake, she stayed on as a cook and washerwoman for the prospectors. It wasn't long before she took in a few boarders, one of whom had had his full of mining and gave her his ten-foot claim as payment for her bill.

Sandy Bowers, another boarder, had his eye on the unmarried Eilley. He proposed. To make matters sweeter, he also held a small claim adjacent to Eilley's. Their marriage produced a rich progeny.

Eilley's predictions from her "peepstone" were coming true; she was becoming a queen. And a queen needed a palace, so she hired stonecutters to build her a magnificent granite-block mansion near Franktown. The cost, not including the imported details and furnishings for the inside, ran between three and four hundred thousand dollars. She spared nothing; the house had horn furniture and marble mantels, Venetian mirrors and lace curtains.

Yearning for acceptance from her family back in Europe and from others living more "civilized" lives, Eilley ventured out, like other rags-to-riches boomtown millionaires, to meet real royalty. She and Sandy traveled to Europe and bent the ear of Charles Francis Adams, who was the U.S. Ambassador to England and, they hoped, their connection to Queen Victoria. But Mrs. Eilley Orrum Bowers was a two-time divorcée, a category unfit for an audience with the queen. Nevertheless, rumors spread about her meeting not only the Queen of England but Napoleon and Empress Eugénie as well.

Whether she hobnobbed with royals or not, Eilley certainly spent like one. Before she left Europe, she had squandered a reported two hundred and fifty thousand dollars on jewels and clothes. Story has it that she also brought back an unusual souvenir from Westminster Abbey: a clipping of ivy for her mansion back home.

The profits from the mine eventually slowed, and coupled with Sandy's death at thirty-eight in 1868, Eilley lost what little status she had—she had never been accepted by the "society" of

The lamp in the store window (opposite) was probably a poor cousin to the chandeliers and other fixtures in the Bowers Mansion (below) in nearby Franktown.

Virginia City—and her fortune. First the mine went, then her furniture, and finally the house (which is now part of a county park). Yet, her odd queenly attitude affected her plans even as she left Washoe. She couldn't bear to leave the ivy clipping for a less appreciative owner and killed it by watering it with a solution of lye.

After her fortune was played out, she settled in as one of the characters of Virginia City. There she was known as the "Washoe Seeress." Her path blurs after that. Perhaps she went on to Reno and San Francisco, perhaps to Oakland. The stories vary, but she never recouped the prosperity she had predicted for herself.

As Eilley Orrum Bowers' fortune rose and fell, four men—"the Lords of Comstock"—made their own fortunes: mining specialists John Mackay and James Fair and saloon keepers James Flood and William O'Brien. Tipped off by talk in their San Francisco establishment, Flood and O'Brien played the stock exchange so well that they built a reputation and a business for themselves that eventually attracted the attention of Mackay and Fair (who had started out as placer miners). Described as opposites, kind, fair-minded Mackay and "Slippery Jim" Fair formed a partnership in Virginia City with the two former barkeeps. Their business acumen and antics yielded from ten to twenty-five million dollars for each man.

Hard work often goes hand in hand with hard play, and one day in 1875, Flood and Fair with their guest H. J. Ramsdell, a reporter from the New York *Tribune*, visited their latest

*V*irginia City's respectability took many forms: as artful details in its cemetery (above and right), in the gingerbread on its Victorian homes, and in the silver bell (made from Comstock bullion) that once hung in its Gothic Catholic church. Divisions between the social classes became marked. While miners toiled, others danced. One social club rounded up all the canaries in town and kept the birds in the dark for days before a dance. The night of the party, the birds sang to the accompaniment of a grand orchestra.

newsworthy accomplishment: the "wooden wonder of the West," a fifteen-mile (24.1-km) V-shaped flume made of two million feet (60 million cm) of lumber and twenty-eight tons (25 metric tons) of nails and spikes.

Before building this flume, wood had been transported on dusty, muddy, and snow-bound roads. Because two fires had burned through the Comstock area, first in 1865 and then again in 1867, each time the townspeople rebuilt they had to go higher and higher into the Sierras for wood since what little timber was around had been used many years before. This flume modernized Comstock mining; it was a vast improvement over dry troughs and square-shaped troughs. The flume height itself was a feat, rising to seventy feet (21.3 m) in places.

So Ramsdell wanted to see the wonder for himself. Somehow Flood, who delighted in the ostentatious, and Fair, who wouldn't be outdone, dared each other to ride the flume. Ramsdell, being a good reporter, couldn't let an opportunity like this pass him by. He joined up. Then John Hereford, the construction boss for the flume, also signed on for the breakneck adventure, probably to keep Ramsdell out of danger.

Like the flume itself, their boats were V-shaped and narrow, just narrow enough to fit comfortably in the watery trough. A board behind served as the back and two more fitted in as seats. The theory was that water would press against the boats and move them forward— fast. Fair and Ramsdell, preparing to get into

This lithograph of the great flume ride depicts what the New York Tribune called a "foolhardy adventure." The Tribune reporter wrote, "It is about fifteen miles in length, leading from a lofty elevation down to the plain, and crossing in its course deep ravines, skirting terrible precipices and chasms, and presenting many sharp curves."

the first boat, paused a moment to ask for a knowledgeable volunteer to travel with them, someone who knew the flume well. (After all, Flood had Hereford with him.) A carpenter accepted the challenge.

No one stopped to think about the physics of the ride—the first boat was heavier in the water, so the two boats would travel at different speeds. They loaded up and took off like luge riders in the Olympics—but with no control. The boats were hurtling down the western wonder with the men pondering their mortality when the first boat struck something that made it buck and throw the carpenter through the air into the water. Fair caught the unfortunate man as the boat broke free, and they all resumed their terrifying ride.

Nearing the end of the flume, the boats caught up with one another and crashed. The seventy-foot (21.3-m) heights and jagged rocks had barely been left behind. Fair, Flood, and the others hastened out of the boats and picked their way down the slope to safety.

2

California

Panamint City

Independence is referred to as a "Deserted Village" as follows:

> *That's the name of our town about these times. A few remain here; some because they are attached to the place much as a rat is to a steel-trap when he can't get away, others because they like a quiet decent time, the remainder because they think this is going to be the best place of all of them after awhile. The main cause may be summed up in one word— Panamint.*

> *—Panamint News, November 26, 1874*

Panamint Valley lies just west of Death Valley; rising up from its floor is the entrance to Surprise Canyon, a broad gravel-laden fan that closes into a narrow cul-de-sac lined by suffocatingly steep cliffs. Legend tells of Charles Alvord and a partner, seekers of a lost mine, who trod the forbidding path. Terrorized by the claustrophobic cliffs, Alvord's partner went crazy and killed him. If they had only continued, the grade rises about a mile (1.6 km) along the cramped path that cuts in twelve miles (19.3 km) farther. The end of the tight canyon opens up into a little valley. Panamint City grew up in these close quarters, well away from the law.

From the very beginning, this "suburb of hell" attracted men who gave the camp one of the worst reputations in all of the West—at least according to Wells Fargo. The Hank Gibbons gang led the way, and their story is inextricably tied to that of two others: Robert Stewart and William Kennedy.

After a few unsuccessful expeditions into the area, Stewart again persuaded Kennedy to put up a grubstake and go exploring with him. They'd been in the Pana-

The chimney of Panamint City's twenty-stamp mill (opposite), which crushed the ore for processing, has survived more than one hundred years. The mill's durability encouraged everyone to believe in the future of Panamint. It was, however, part of an elaborate hoax. The owners of the mines held onto their stock just long enough to become masters of the mill, where the real profit was to be made, since much of the mine's ore came from rich surface deposits.

mints before and had seen enough to want to go back. In the autumn of 1872, they met their guardian angel in the guise of a well-worn, be-whiskered forty-niner named Richard Jacobs. Jacobs guided them to an area where he had picked up some promising float, a chunk of rock that comes—but has been separated—from an ore-bearing lode. Landslides, erosion, and downpours can all push the float down and away from its source. Many lucky prospectors located rich mines by following up on float.

Their treasure hunt took them to the small valley at the rear of the canyon. The change in topography was so unexpected that they named the entire canyon "Surprise Canyon."

That December, the three men found the quartz lodes they were looking for—just above the future town site. Not wanting to get caught in the winter snows, they packed up some ore for the assayer and left for Kernville, the location of Kennedy's store. They had indeed found a strike; they didn't wait to go back. Instead, they loaded up with food and supplies and returned to the Panamints almost immediately. Although they couldn't get through to Surprise Canyon, they got close enough to set up camp and wait for the thaw.

It didn't take long for them to realize they were being followed. Little did they know that the six desperadoes behind them were a known—and feared—gang. Led by Hank Gibbons, the gunmen had held up a Wells Fargo stage and were traveling southwest from Pioche to take cover in the Panamints.

Jacobs and the others tried to throw them off the scent with no luck. Claim jumpers they most surely were. But were they killers too? No one knew. The three prospectors gambled with their lives; they convinced the con men that there was enough good land for everyone. Ironically, one of Gibbons' gang claimed the biggest-earning mine site.

Word spread quickly, and single-blanket jackass prospectors shared quarters with gangs of surly men wanted by the law. The homicide rate rivaled the rowdiest camps. Out of necessity, the citizens co-opted the two-wheeled butcher's cart to use as a hearse, ferrying the shoot-out victims to the newly plotted boot hill in Sour Dough Gulch. This didn't stop the miners from later carrying Lady Liberty and three little girls in the cart as it floated down the main street on the Fourth of July.

When the mines began producing, the man-

Before Panamint City sprang up (opposite page, top 1877, and bottom 1991), the town site, up the path from Surprise Canyon (above), accommodated a tent camp centered around miner Richard Jacobs' tent nicknamed the Hotel de Bum.

agers asked Wells Fargo to carry the Panamint silver safely out of town and out of the canyon. Thanks to a little under-the-table maneuvering—and a small fortune from selling their mines to two Nevada senators—the Gibbons gang bought their respectability. Apparently they paid back Wells Fargo with interest, and the company conveniently forgot that the gang had ever robbed their stage, but they still wouldn't agree to service the town. The Gibbons gang may have changed their tune, but there were plenty of others lurking in the caves and ramshackle shacks of the canyon.

Thumbing their noses at the established company, Senator William Stewart and the mining managers decided to take the silver out of the canyon unescorted. Not one armed guard accompanied the open wagons, and when the freighters got to a critical corner, highwaymen ambushed them. The driver stepped down and said, "Help yourselves, boys!" But the thieves couldn't steal a thing because the silver was cast into 750-pound cannonballs. So the story goes. (Although in truth, the silver made it out of the canyon as 400-pound cubes, which were still large enough to foil all attempted robberies.)

Upholding its reputation, Panamint boasted about two dozen bars in less than a mile (1.6 km). "The saloon was a place of congregation. Men gathered to it as primitive men gathered about the fire," wrote Jack London. Like its larger sister, Virginia City, Panamint had a number of chandeliered, elegant bars and restaurants with oysters on the menu. The growing community of rich miners craved a little luxury. The Dexter Saloon was only too happy to comply. It hoped to outdo its nearby competitors, Neagle's Oriental Saloon and the Occidental, by bringing round the Horn a seven-by-twelve-foot (2.13 - by - 3.66 m) mirror to put behind the bar.

When it reached the mainland, the showpiece traveled by mule team to Panamint City. It was such an oddity that the townspeople crowded into the canyon a mile (1.6 km) back to accompany the freighter as it brought its load into town. But as the men carried the mirror into the saloon, they stumbled, and the silvered glass fell with a shattering crash.

Perhaps the broken mirror brought the town bad luck, because the once-roaring camp didn't last long. Panamint peaked for only four years before it too crashed. The paper had already closed down and the majority of the miners had scattered when a terrific rainstorm hit the mountains above the forsaken city. The remaining townspeople could hear the roar of the water before it came rushing down the main street—with waves as high as fifty feet (15.2 m). The wall of water took down most of what was left, and in its wake, fifteen citizens lay dead. Even the outlaws abandoned the canyon.

Skidoo

Up the hills from Ballarat some forty miles or more,
The man who made the Panamints, he left a ledge of ore;
The man who made the Panamints had something on his
*   mind,*
He left the ledge of ore in sight for you and me to
*   find;*
It's forty miles from Ballarat, the mountains there are
*   blue,*
The place is numbered twenty-three, they've named the
*   spot Skidoo!*
                    —from the *Death Valley Chuckwalla,*
                        February 15, 1907

Locals call the tight gorge in Surprise Canyon "the Narrows" (opposite). A few people still live around Surprise Canyon, including the owners of the Panamint town site, who leased their rights in the 1980s to a rancher who poured five million dollars into the land before retreating. The area maintains its reputation for wildness, and trespassers are not always welcome. With the exception of the hanging of "Hootch" Simpson, Skidoo and environs (left) was known for its good humor. Both Panamint City and Skidoo edge the boundaries of Death Valley National Monument.

Skidoo was a baby boomer, a scratch on the surface of western mining lore, but it left its mark through its odd name and an even odder occurrence.

The baptismal story begins with two old pros, John Ramsey and John "One-Eye" Thompson, above the Emigrant Canyon Springs in the mountains along the western part of Death Valley. The two prospectors were forced to stop because of fog, a rarity in those parts. Prospectors weren't known to twiddle their thumbs even in a fog, so the delay merely gave them a little time to look around. And it's fortunate they did. They stumbled on some float that led them to a lode big enough to absorb thirty claims.

It wasn't that they kept it a secret. It's just that they didn't leave. Nor did the others who happened to find them. Everyone wanted a piece of the rock. They made their claims and started working them immediately.

Three months later, the two discoverers optioned their best twenty-three claims for twenty-three thousand dollars. The buyer's wife exclaimed, "twenty-three skidoo," and the town was named. So one story goes.

Another recounts the building of a water pipeline that supposedly ran twenty-three miles (37 km) from its source on Telescope Peak to the Skidoo Mine. Yet another story maintains that the town was founded on the twenty-third of the month. The *Chuckwalla* sums it up nicely: "The man who named the town may have been a humorist, he may have

Souvenir hunters have ravaged the town site of Skidoo, which once housed seven hundred people in more than a hundred buildings. Nothing is left of the houses that once sat on thousand-dollar lots or of the mill (opposite, taken in 1907), only of the mining operations. The ore loader and car (opposite, inset) and the pylons by the mine entrance (above) are among the best-preserved artifacts.

Skidoo grew because it stood closest to the Skidoo mine. Bob Montgomery, who developed the mine, wanted to name the town after himself. The post office wanted to name it after Montgomery's manager, Matt Hoveck. But the people insisted on Skidoo, which became official on April Fool's Day of 1907. The Skidoo mine was a profitable venture, earning its owner a 50 percent profit even though the town felt the financial panic of 1907. It went on to pay dividends to its stockholders for many years. The ore loader (right) stands as a memorial to the mine's success.

been satirical or wanted to be; on the desert it is always difficult to discern the motive that suggested the name for a place, but certainly the name has been anything but hoodoo."

Hoodoo, indeed. Skidoo brought good luck to most of its citizens. Unlike its neighbor, Panamint City, Skidoo remained peaceful and law-abiding. Its boss, Bob Montgomery, believed in the mines and used much of his own money to make a go of it. In the end, the Skidoo mines paid dividends to its stockholders, an event as rare as the fog that initially stopped Ramsey and Thompson.

News came and went by heliograph, a telegraph that worked by flashing the sun's rays from a mirror to another spot: in this case, across Death Valley to Rhyolite. But there was not much to report except mining dispatches, that is, until April 19, 1908.

April nineteenth was Easter Sunday morning, and Joe "Hootch" Simpson, a questionable character with unappreciated bravado, had been on a bender. Hootch had been there when Skidoo shot up from the rough-hewn landscape, but that didn't make anyone like him any better. He was a mean and nasty drunk, whose behavior some people say was exacerbated by syphilis-induced rantings. And he wasn't kidding around that day. As the *Skidoo News* told it on April 25:

"Hootch" . . . had been indulging in his favorite stimulant for some days and was in a highly inflamed state. Joe was out of funds, a

condition not calculated to improve his usual, bad temper, and to his disordered imagination, the only practical way of getting it was to kill a banker.

The gun-toting fool headed into the Skidoo Trading Company, a general store that housed a counter for the Southern California Bank. Hootch had it in his mind to rob the bank. Pointing his gun at the cashier, he demanded twenty dollars; before any damage could be done, Jim Arnold, who owned the store, physically threw Simpson off the premises.

Since Skidoo had no jail, the sheriff wanted to cuff Simpson to a telephone pole until a warrant could be obtained from nearby Independence. Instead, the drunk voluntarily took to bed and fell asleep in the custody of his partner, a man named Oakes, who hid Simpson's gun in the oven. Oakes left to take care of business in the saloon he ran with Simpson. Simpson meanwhile awakened with a bad hangover and a bruised ego. It didn't take him long to find the hidden gun. He strode into the store once more and, according to the *Skidoo News*:

> *. . . passed the bank counter and approaching Jim Arnold asked, "Have you got anything against me, Jim?" and Arnold answered, "No, Joe, I've got nothing against you." "Yes you have—your end has come—prepare to die!" And with that he raised his gun and shot Arnold below the heart.*

Now in many frontier towns, shootings were status quo. When the shooter was brought be-

fore a judge, the judge declared self-defense, and the criminal walked away free. Simpson's jury, however, convicted him. But the Skidoovians were a community-minded bunch, and they had liked Jim Arnold. Rather than strain the coffers of the county—by putting Simpson through the court and prison systems—they took matters into their own hands. Strangely enough, when asked, no one knew anything about how Simpson ended up hanging from a telephone pole the next morning.

The news traveled fast that old Hootch Simpson had been hung and was apparently still swinging from the pole as a warning to other lawbreakers. Journalists and photographers rushed to the sight, but Simpson had been buried. Taking it in stride, the Skidoovians simply dug him up, dusted the body off, and strung him up again.

That's the legend. The "truth" is almost as strange. A Dr. Macdonald took photos of Hootch before the burial. After the burial, he took a little more than photos. In fact, he went back and cut off Simpson's head. All the better to study his brain. But the poor man's head didn't find its way to the grave. Instead, it rested on an anthill for a bit before the good doctor boiled it in an attempt to clean it up for display.

Skidoo died a slower, quieter death. Although the pipeline laid the ground for a potentially successful town site and the residents no longer had to take tomato-can baths, the financial panic that hit the nation in October 1907 also hit this small, isolated camp. Ever true to its image, Skidoo declined in good humor. As businesses were closing and Skidoovians were leaving, the town threw a "Hard Times Frolic"—complete with entertainment including a herd of performing goats and trained fleas. What little remains is a scar on the earth and a haven for wild burros.

This photo (below), taken in 1916, shows Skidoo at the end of its life. One year later, the mines shut down. In its heyday, the town had been described by one reporter as growing "in a flat little hollow, but it did not nestle because a mining camp does not nestle. Like a tin can, it lies where it is thrown."

Skidoo. It's one of those words that nags the memory. You know you've heard it, but do you really know what it means? Not quite as bad as *scat*, it simply means "go away" or "depart." *Webster's*, which dates it to 1903, traces it to *skedaddle*, a more insistent word that conveys the urgency of fleeing in a panic. (Scholar and author Richard Lingenfelter links it back to the Greek *skedannumi*, which suggests "a riotous retreat.") Not the friendliest name for a town practically lost in the boondocks.

Supposedly a racetrack owner married "twenty-three" to "skidoo." Only twenty-two horses could race on his track. When subsequent entrants asked for admission, he'd reply, "Twenty-three for you, Skidoo!" and turn them away. From there it caught on with the swell set and vaudeville.

3

New Mexico
ghost towns

Shakespeare

Good friend, for Jesus' sake forbear
To dig the dust enclosed here;
Blest be the man that spares these stones,
And curst be he that moves my bones.
—Shakespeare's *Epitaph*

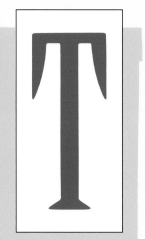

There may not have been a theater in Shakespeare—Shakespeare, New Mexico, that is—but there was always plenty of drama. Tragedies and comedies alike played out in hard-tack reality by prostitutes and prospectors, minstrels and mountain men, Apaches and pioneers. Shakespeare. The fancy tag conjures up a loud, literary tribute to England for a quiet, haunted American town. But the story behind the name is the story behind the town itself.

Situated just south of the dust-bedeviled Pyramid Mountains, facing east toward Soldier's Farewell and pointing west toward Doubtful Canyon, the town that eventually became known as Shakespeare began as a watering hole for the Apaches. Apaches camped there, pioneers and fortune seekers on their way to California filled their jugs there, and mountain men and freighters passed through. Back when Shakespeare was called Mexican Spring, which was in or about 1856, someone—no one knows who—slapped together an adobe building on the site. Like the latest club in town (a watering hole in the desert!), everybody who needed to know knew about

Scenes of Chloride,
New Mexico (opposite).

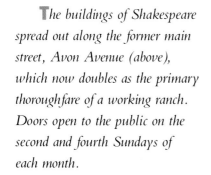

*T*he buildings of Shakespeare spread out along the former main street, Avon Avenue (above), which now doubles as the primary thoroughfare of a working ranch. Doors open to the public on the second and fourth Sundays of each month.

A ghost is said to inhabit the general store (left), which has been converted into a house. The ghost rises from the basement, some say, cloaked in sulfur fumes. And if there's not a ghost in the old Grant House Saloon (below), there should be. The main cross timber served as a hanging post for lawless men. Bullet holes pock the thick walls in the saloon but not from illegal doings; drunks commonly shot at flies on the walls.

Mexican Spring. A year later, in 1857, a stage stop was built when the government's postmaster general selected a mail route from Missouri to Southern California that included Mexican Spring. The route, which was often derogatorily called the "Oxbow Route" because it bent out one thousand miles (1609 km) longer than the direct route from St. Louis to San Francisco, was supposed to be a more passable and easily traveled trail.

When the Civil War broke out, however, the stage stopped passing through Mexican Spring. During the war, a group of Confederate soldiers occupied the old adobe structure and prepared it for a Union attack, but the only thing to ever

attack the soldiers at that desolate spring was a mean and mind-bending case of thumb twiddling. So the soldiers went home, leaving Mexican Spring to the tumbleweeds—until the war ended and "Uncle Johnny" Evenson came upon the scene.

Uncle Johnny, who was also called "Jack Frost" in some circles, opened a new stage station at Mexican Spring in 1867 when he was fifty-three years old. Over the years he was there, the town boomed, busted, boomed again, and busted, and through it all, Uncle Johnny remained, along with one other fella whose name has been lost to time. And so, Uncle Johnny—or someone at the time—decided to rename the town Grant. Whether he didn't like the word *Mexican* in Mexican Spring or he was a fan of Ulysses S. Grant (a popular figure at the time) and trying to hide the town's Confederate past, no one knows for sure, but Grant it was and Grant House was the name chosen for the main adobe building in town.

When a prospector named W. D. Brown passed through and found silver in the Pyramid Mountains near Grant, the quiet lives of Uncle Johnny and his friend changed for good. Brown, who had barely escaped the area with his scalp intact, took the ore to San Francisco to be assayed. Some of it measured twelve thousand ounces (340 kg) to the ton, which sparked the interest of one William C. Ralston. Ralston was a millionaire mining tycoon and founder of the Bank of California. He and some of his men beat a path to the town of Grant so

hard and dry it could have cut out a canyon. In 1870, they plotted out a town around Uncle Johnny's stage station, staked hundreds of claims left and right, and renamed the town Ralston City.

Ralston, the man, organized his claims into the New Mexico Mining Company and wasted no time selling stock in the venture all over Europe. To protect his interests, he hired a small, private army to enforce the law. Now a booming town of a few hundred people, fights broke out frequently in Ralston City. There were no wives or children at this time, only bachelor miners, claim jumpers, and whores. Gradually these inexperienced souls realized that the ore could be found only in small pockets, and even then, it was low grade. When that happened, Ralston City went bust for the first time.

Ralston tried to leave town quietly to keep his stock from falling rapidly, but others caught on quickly and began to leave, until there was no one left except—of course—Uncle Johnny.

Empty, dusty, and forsaken, life in Ralston City was like déjà vu for Uncle Johnny until two men by the names of Philip Arnold and John Slack claimed they discovered diamonds there. (Arnold was one of the miners who had originally guided Ralston and his men into the Pyramid Mountains for silver.) The two men checked in a sack of diamonds at an assay office in San Francisco, knowing full well Ralston would find out about it. A few of the stones had been appraised at one hundred and fifty thousand dollars. Ralston paid Arnold and Slack six hundred thousand dollars to tell him where the site was. Ralston kept the location secret and never heard from Arnold and Slack again.

Secrets don't last long in mining country, however, and soon Ralston City boomed again—this time to three thousand people. There were stores and restaurants, seven saloons, an assay office, a Chinese laundry, and boarding houses. Diamonds in New Mexico! It was almost too good to be true. And indeed it was. It took only a few words from a government geologist to set the record straight and to set Ralston City on its back again. "This is the greatest field ever," he is remembered to have said, "for it not only produces diamonds for us to find but it cuts them yet." Arnold and Slack had "salted" the field with a few genuine cut diamonds and dozens of phony ones. Ralston went bankrupt and later drowned himself in San Francisco Bay, and in 1875, Ralston City turned ghost town once more.

Now with the reputation as a town of fraud and deceit, Ralston City became a frequent stopover for outlaws. It was not until 1879, when two St. Louis gentlemen of English descent bought up what was left of the gold and silver claims in the Pyramid Mountains, that the town became "respectable" once more. Colonel John Boyle, a Shakespearean scholar, and his brother William renamed the town after John's literary hero, Shakespeare. Main Street became Avon Avenue and Grant House, updated and refurbished, became the Stratford Hotel.

Although it professed an air of respectability (the hookers were escorted out of town each morning), Shakespeare had its share of rowdies and eccentric citizens. For example, the manager of the Stratford Hotel, "Beanbelly" Smith, had a run-in in his very own place of business when his staff refused to serve him an egg for breakfast. It seems that at the table next to him, a man named Ross Woods, who ran the National Mail and Transportation Company and who was staying at the hotel, ordered an egg and got one. Beanbelly started an argument not with his staff but with Woods, who ran upstairs and came back down with guns ablaze. Beanbelly shot him, sat down, and ate Woods' egg.

Woods became the first customer at Shakespeare's cemetery. Outlaw "Curly" Bill Brocius, who was famous for his bright red neckties, had died earlier, but he didn't have time to

Billy the Kid supposedly washed dishes at the Stratford Hotel (above) in Shakespeare before he earned his gun-totin' reputation. Although the town attracted its share of outlaws, some of its "law-abiding" citizenry perpetrated one of its worst crimes. One day during Prohibition, two black miners who were running a successful operation stopped in the Grant House café, drank a little too much, and agreed to gamble. Their fellow players got angry when the miners won and a chase ensued. The losers caught up with the winners in an arroyo, or gully, that to this day is called the "Arroyo de los Negros" because it was there that the black men were beaten to death by the citizens of Shakespeare.

The interior of the Stratford Hotel (above) maintains the atmosphere of the latter half of the 1800s. Two rooms upstairs have been fixed up to look as they might have in the past. One, outfitted with a wooden bed laced with cowhide and topped with a straw mattress, reflects the 1870s. The other boasts metal-spring beds of the eighties and nineties that were transported to Shakespeare after the railroad was established nearby.

make it to boot hill. Story goes that Wyatt Earp shot him in the stomach, and Curly Bill crawled back to Shakespeare but only made it as far as the general store. They buried him there in the basement. At least people say it's Curly Bill who's buried there.

Tall, with long blonde hair, sparkling spurs, and fancy boots, Russian Bill clanked into town one day dragging with him a supposedly dangerous past. But as time went on and Russian Bill showed no signs of criminal behavior, citizens and outlaws alike grew suspicious of his "notorious" reputation. To squelch the rumors, Russian Bill tried hanging out with a real outlaw—Curly Bill—who was still alive at that time. When Russian Bill rode up to meet

him, Curly Bill shot off the end of Russian Bill's cigar. They spent some time together, but guilt by association didn't cut it for the citizens of Shakespeare. So Russian Bill went out and stole a horse. He was hung for it, of course, from a beam at the Stratford Hotel, along with the long-established outlaw Sandy King, whose crimes were so many that he was finally hung for being "a damned nuisance."

The Roxy Jay saloon served as both a watering hole and a favorite meeting place (and sometimes hanging place) of the vigilante committee and the vigilante court. It was here that the committee tried to hang one Arkansas Black, who was accused of being popular with the ladies and especially intimate with the married wife of a particular miner. Arkansas Black was a handsome devil, a gambler, and a popular man around Shakespeare, but the townspeople got upset over his repeated and blatant mid-afternoon indiscretions. They captured him with the intention of hanging him. Black was outraged, cursed them up and down, and promised to take them on one by one once he got free of his rope necktie. When the chair was kicked out from under him, Black hung for a few seconds before someone cut the rope. He fell to the floor unconscious. They revived him with a bucket of water, remembered how much they liked him, and ran the wife and her husband out of town instead.

So it goes in the town of Shakespeare. And so, it went.

Chloride

Hellish Murder

RED DEVILS AT THEIR BLOODY WORK
TWO OF CHLORIDE'S MINERS RUTHLESSLY MURDERED
BY INDIANS

—headline, *Chloride Black Range*, Sept. 19, 1890

There are some boot hills in ghost towns with headstones for people who never even lived, let alone died. The tiny town of Chloride, New Mexico, however, wasn't capable of telling such lies. Chloride's reputation didn't rest on legends; its claim to fame was its ordinariness.

Located in the foothills of the Black Range in piñon country, about 30 miles (48 km) northwest of Truth or Consequences, Chloride was ordinary in that it had an average number of outlaws, an average number of Apache raids, and an average amount of success from its mines. There were no great bonanzas and no excessive rowdiness—that is, if you accept "hellish murder" as the order of the day, which is how many prairie-worn pioneers looked at life back then.

In 1879, a mule skinner by the name of Harry Pye, who formerly had freighted goods for the U.S. Army, struck his pick into some rock in a narrow Black Range canyon and came up with a rich deposit of silver chloride. Despite the ever-present threat of Indian attacks, Pye returned to the site with some of his friends. They found the mother lode, staked a

*A*t ninety-four, Raymond Schmidt (left), Chloride's oldest resident in 1991, keeps a log book listing all the visitors who pass through the town. He was a noted amateur astronomer in his sprier days and is especially proud that astronauts have come to call on him. His father also had a scientific bent: Henry Schmidt chronicled his time, using photography as his medium. The picture of Chloride's main street (above) was taken by Henry Schmidt circa 1890.

claim that they called the Pye Lode, and thus began the town called Chloride. Simple, and it would have been as easy as pie, except that the Apaches, led by Chief Nana, were on the warpath. It seemed only a matter of time before Harry Pye was picked off in one of the many ambushes and raids common at the time.

Dieffenderfer) were often rumored to be menacingly close to Chloride.

But on the whole, it was business as usual. As recently as 1991, a man named Raymond Schmidt, whose father, Henry Schmidt, had been Chloride's surveyor, assayer, and photographer, still lived in Chloride, along with

Henry Schmidt also took this view of Chloride (opposite, bottom) looking southeast, circa 1890–95. Chloride in 1991 (opposite, top) is gaining new ground. In addition to the few old-timers who remain, recent retirees, attracted to the quiet and the beauty of the area, are resettling there. The old stone houses (left) at the southeast end of the main street date back to the 1920s. They were supposedly built by a cousin of Captain Jack, the New Mexican folk hero known as the "Poet Scout."

In 1881, there were fifty people living in Chloride. By 1883, the population grew to two thousand. In its heyday, Chloride boasted a newspaper, a hotel, a bakery, a drugstore, several saloons, and a one-room schoolhouse with a potbellied stove. Every Saturday night there was a dance and every Sunday morning a court was held to square what had happened the week before. Outlaws "Rattlesnake Jack" and "Buckskin Bob" (whose real name was Billy

twenty-seven other people. True to Chloride's everything-in-moderation past, Schmidt remembered the stories of both the good and the bad: Chloride's 1888 Fourth of July sported four horse races, a shooting match, and a baseball game played against nearby Fairview that was cut to five innings due to darkness. Chloride won. And the time "three gay and festive cowboys" named Harry Froehlich, Harry Reilly, and William Hardin shot up the town. Or the

The White Eagle Mine in February 1891 (above) shows the crude mechanisms that launched many a mining operation and many a town. This is another example of Henry Schmidt's work, one of two thousand prints extant.

time Schmidt and his brother came home one day to find a bobcat in the house. Figuring he'd take the wiser path, Schmidt stepped aside to let his brother grab a club and go inside to "fix" the bobcat but good. What got fixed was Schmidt's brother, who fell through the door with the bobcat leaping over him and off into the night.

It took a lot to scare a Chloride citizen. Apaches usually did the trick better than outlaws. At that time, Apaches were thought of as "red fiends of hell," "marauding hostiles" who performed "dastardly outrages." The white settlers were often hostile to the Indians, and the Indians often struck back. Apaches were re-

sponsible for the oft-told story of the death of Oscar Pfotenhauer, who was shot in the back while he was working the Unknown Mine. His partner hid in the shaft until he could run down the gulch for help. With armed men in tow, the partner followed an Apache trail to the Silver Monument Mine only to find that they were too late. Yet another Chloride miner was dead.

Chloride hasn't quite died. Although nature can make short work of abandoned structures, the care and concern of just a few people can keep a town alive. Retirees are moving in, giving the town another push, but it's the stories as much as the population that bring Chloride to life.

Cabezon

What mysteries do lie beyond thy dust . . .
—Henry Vaughan, *They Are All Gone*, 1655

The hollow homes and crumbling stores of the near-empty village of Cabezon, New Mexico, epitomize the loneliness one always finds in the streets of a true ghost town. Ageless Cabezon is running its race against time, although three families still make their homes there. Adaptation has kept the town somewhat intact. One resident stores his hay in the church, the front door barricaded with an old coil-spring mattress to keep the goats out.

Unlike other ghost towns, Cabezon didn't boom overnight and wasn't born as a result of a lone prospector and his scruffy burro striking gold. Cabezon has been around longer than the United States has been a nation, and its history stretches back to before white men entered the area. There were Indian adobe villages with small, sacred mud rooms tucked into the base of Cabezon Peak, with painted murals inside made by a people long dead but not forgotten. They lived along the Rio Puerco probably as early as the Vikings landed on the Atlantic coast of North America.

To the Navajo, Cabezon means Big Head, and Cabezon Peak, a towering volcanic plug rising to more than seven thousand feet (2133 m), is the head of a giant killed by Navajo folk heroes, the Twin War Brothers. The lava-scarred gouges flowing down to the peak's

What's left of the town of *Cabezon lies on private property. The long driveway to the old adobe buildings (previous page) was once the main street of town. With so few inhabitants, Cabezon feels eerily abandoned, as if someone from the past is still watching the town. Electricity doesn't exist here, and water for the animals comes from a well many miles away. One of the residents lamented that the young people had all moved away, lured by the promise of refrigerators and television sets. The highway is about fifteen minutes away, but Cabezon Peak (right) stands hidden from the rush of traffic.*

base represent the giant's clotted blood. The Rio Puerco is part of a sacred boundary to the Navajo people. Rio Puerco means Muddy River, and the section that passes by Cabezon is often so dry and rocky it seems to have been carved out by the sun.

The Spanish exploited the area of Cabezon beginning in the 1500s. They grew maize, beans, pumpkins, and wheat, and tended cattle and goats. By the 1760s, non-native settlers were living at the base of the mountain. As the settlement grew, groups of houses sprang up on the banks of the river. There was a church and a few stores. Indians repeatedly attacked the settlers, but over time, they gave up.

By 1863, largely due to the efforts of Colonel Kit Carson, the Indians were defeated and white settlers became entrenched. William Kanzenback and Rudolph Haberland opened a store and a saloon. In 1875, the Star Line Mail stagecoach made a stop at Cabezon. During its peak years, Cabezon had a church, a restaurant, four stores, a rooming house, and a few saloons. When the railroad decided not to pass through the town, however, Cabezon moved closer and closer toward its demise.

Before it died, however, Cabezon contributed its fair share of ghost town tales. One cowboy, it is said, developed a habit of riding his horse inside saloons and dance halls. Once he rode right into the schoolhouse and lassoed the teacher. An old man living on the banks of the Rio Puerco supposedly buried some gold under a fence post, and it is rumored to be there still.

Unlike many of the rowdy camps of the West, E-town's population included a fair number of women and children. Getting gold safely out of town was often a problem in even the quietest communities, but in E-town where crime was not unheard of, kids came to the rescue, at least in one family. Story has it that the children acted as couriers with thousands of dollars worth of gold nuggets wrapped in their pockets. If the stage was robbed, no one would bother with the kids. The few structures left in E-town (opposite) are best remembered by the characters who frequented them.

But the most excitement Cabezon generated came from an ax murder, although there wasn't much mystery surrounding who actually did the dirty deed. A postal inspector came to town to check up on the postmaster and the whereabouts of some missing money. The inspector questioned a man named Juan Valdez. Valdez didn't exactly tell on the postmaster, he simply shrugged in agreement, apparently confirming the inspector's suspicions. Not impressed by the way Valdez handled himself during the questioning, the residents of Cabezon rode up to his house and axed Valdez to death.

The Rio Puerco was a dry and isolated valley, making it ideal for outlaws and Mexican banditos. The brothers Candido and Manuel Castillo were notorious cattle rustlers who frequently plagued the area. Having had enough, a posse was organized and chased the duo up into the hills. They were barely able to slow the bandits down until they finally found them holed up in an abandoned ranch house. A blazing shoot-out ensued near the corral, but the posse still couldn't put an end to the brothers. Following their bloody tracks in the snow, the posse eventually traced them to the Penitente Brotherhood. The brothers were members of this mysterious religious sect, which held secret Holy Week rites that were said to include real-life reenactments of the crucifixion of Christ. To put it plainly, the posse turned back. And the Castillo brothers were never heard from again.

Elizabethtown

May thy wheels never turn without profit to thy owners; may there be no loss of gold in thy boxes; no leakage of water in thy seams. May harmony and success prevail. May our kind host gather wealth and comfort from thee and ever continue to be one of us—a good fellow.

—from Mrs. Mougey's speech christening the Reisling E-town dredge, 1901

The money, the greed, and the killing all began for Elizabethtown in 1866 when an Indian trader arrived at Fort Union and showed two men—W. H. Kroenig and William Moore—a couple of "pretty rocks" he had brought along with his skins. Kroenig and Moore convinced the Indian to show them where he found the rocks, which led the two men to start the Mystic Copper Mine at the foot of Baldy Mountain. Later that year, a group of prospectors also from Fort Union found gold in a ten-mile (16 km) placer field at nearby Willow Creek. Gold quickly became the fever of the moment, and copper was ignored. It was only a matter of days before men were swarming over the land to lay claims. Three hundred men quit their posts at Fort Union to seek their fortunes in gold.

The main settlement sprang up in the area at the base of Baldy Mountain in the Moreno Valley about five miles (8 km) north of Eagle Nest Lake. Initially called Virginia City, it was soon renamed Elizabethtown, in honor of Elizabeth Caterina, surveyor Captain John Moore's daughter. The long name was immediately shortened, of course, by the impatient tongues of the money-hungry miners, and Elizabethtown became commonly known as E-town.

By 1868, E-town's population had passed five hundred and grown to an astounding seven thousand. Three stagecoach lines passed through E-town and brought business to the seven saloons, five stores, drugstore, newspaper, two hotels, and three dance halls. The town was most productive from '68 to '69 when almost five million dollars' worth of gold was recovered. As the town grew, however, it was in desperate need of water. Two businessmen named Maxwell and Davis, from Fort Union and Las Vegas respectively, began construction of forty-two miles (68 km) of ditches to bring water to E-town. Known as the Big Ditch, the system was completed in 1868 to the tune of $280,000, and the first water was delivered to Humbug Gulch on July 9, 1869. Unfortunately, the Big Ditch only scratched the surface of E-town's ongoing water woes.

The size of E-town's population was matched only by the enormity of its violent day-to-day atmosphere. A Mexican spending some time in the E-town jail requested and received a change of venue through the proper channels of the law—only to be dragged from his cell by vigilantes. They hung him from the rafters and stuck a calling card on his shirt that read, "So much for the change of venue."

The miners who built these stone walls (right) also hammered five miles through Baldy Mountain, using only a simple hand drill. They found gold on the hillside and in the placer streams. Seemingly, there was room enough for everyone, but E-town became famous for its vigilantes, some of whom killed as easily as outlaws.

A vigilante committee was set up to capture the bad guys and protect the good, but it often accomplished the opposite instead. During a committee meeting in a dark back room, a cigar box of marked chips—each one scratched with the name of a local outlaw—was passed around from man to man. Whichever name the vigilante drew he'd have to remember forever, because one day he could be asked to kill the marked man. One saloonkeeper, Joseph Herberger, used the vigilante committee to rid the town of his personal enemies. His lies about an innocent man named Pony O'Neil ended O'Neil's life. Herberger also shot a man, a rival saloon keeper named George Greeley of George's Place, for throwing a more successful dance on Saturday night than Herberger had had at his place. Although Herberger was sent to the Sante Fe penitentiary for that murder, he

later returned to E-town where he died of a heart attack.

E-town was a rough place where story has it that eight people died within a single twenty-four-hour period. One ex-prospector-turned-hoodlum named Wall Henderson specialized in killing people by shooting them in the eye. His six-gun was notched eight times on one side for the men he had wounded and seven on the other for the ones he had killed. One time, when a young criminal lawyer named Melvin Mills came to E-town, Henderson shot a man dead at Mills' feet, then forced him at gunpoint to sign a paper saying he'd never prosecute Henderson for the shooting or any other crimes he might want to commit. Henderson was inevitably shot down in a barroom brawl.

By the midseventies, placers were wearing thin, Indians were causing problems, settlers were drifting away, and outlaws continued to run wild. Counselor Mills had his work cut out for him. "Coal Oil Johnny" (or "Jimmy," as he was also known) and "Long Tom" Taylor were notorious for robbing stagecoaches. A price of three thousand dollars was put on their heads. Two other lesser-known outlaws, Joe McCurdy and John Stewart, wanted to collect the reward. They joined Coal Oil Johnny's gang in order to capture them and kill them. McCurdy and Stewart made a pact with lawyer Mills to collect the reward. They no sooner shook hands on the deal than McCurdy and Stewart pulled the cover off their buckboard showing Mills the corpses of Coal Oil Johnny and Long Tom Taylor. McCurdy and Stewart got the reward.

The most gruesome and bizarre story to ever come out of E-town was surprisingly enough lawyer Mills' first case. It all started when a Mexican woman, who most recognized as Charles Kennedy's wife, burst into a saloon with her feet bleeding and raving about how her husband had been killing their children and anyone else who stopped off at their inn. A group of men rode out to the Kennedy place only to find him burning the bones of a drifter who had stopped off for some water and a bite to eat. Apparently, Kennedy was running a latter-day Bates Motel, luring travelers inside, murdering them, and then putting their bodies under his floorboards until he had the chance to either burn or bury them. The story goes that one traveler, while seated at the dinner table with the Mexican wife and a child, asked

Kennedy if there were any Indians about. The child answered, "Can't you smell the one Papa put under the floor?" Kennedy shot the guest, bashed the brains out of the little boy, locked the woman in a closet, and passed out drunk. The woman broke out of the closet and escaped up the chimney.

Melvin Mills defended Kennedy, and the trial resulted in a hung jury. But some of the townspeople yanked Kennedy from his cell and dragged him through the streets by the neck until he was dead. Some say an unsavory character by the name of Clay Allison cut off Kennedy's head and got a good price for it a few towns over. Others say the head had a strange shape and was sent to the Smithsonian Institution for study.

It wasn't until H. J. Reisling's enormous dredge that E-town actually boomed again. A monstrosity of machinery with boilers weighing twenty-one thousand pounds (7833 kg) each, the dredge was too fearsome to be moved, but Jack Bennett and Charles Webber decided to try anyway. They widened the roads, built special bridges, and arrived in E-town with the big boat. Christened on August 20, 1901, by a Mrs. Mougey from Ohio, the dredge was the subject of much political fanfare. For four years, the dredge worked two shifts of men a day and paid for itself within the year. It was later mortgaged, however, and the new owners let the dredge sink to the bottom until eventually the mechanical beast that brought so much hope completely disappeared.

4. Colorado

Grand Lake Area

*It is quite cold here o' nights, and we have some threaten-
ings of snow. There is an awful surplusage of ventilation about
our cabin, and I have nightly misgivings that I shall be blown
through the cracks, but Providence watches over us all.*
—from a letter printed in *Rocky Mountain News*, 1859

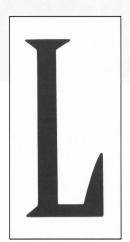

Located in the northwestern part of the state, some one hundred miles northwest of Denver in what was Arapaho Indian country, Grand Lake today marks the western border of Rocky Mountain National Park. The glacial lake dates from prehistoric times; its constant blue color contrasts with the thick, deep-green pine-bordered shores. It is said that some of its waters are so deep they've never been plumbed.

Long before white men ever came to the Grand Lake region, a fierce battle took place between the Arapaho and Ute Indian tribes that in its way foretold the area's tragic and often bizarre future.

Grand Lake was a favorite camping ground of the Ute. When they came under attack from the Arapaho, they quickly set their women and children afloat on makeshift barges and rafts. The lake should have offered them protection, but it didn't. As the story goes, during the battle a storm came on suddenly and sent hundreds of innocent people to their deaths at the bottom of the lake. From that moment on, the Ute hated the area and believed that the mists rising up from Grand Lake were the spirits of the Unfortunates.

Creede bustled with activity in the early 1890s (opposite). One hundred hotels catered to the miners and their followers. Today (opposite, inset) only the Creede Hotel stands, but it is carrying on the traditions of a good small hotel.

Bad luck seemed to haunt everyone who made their way to the region during the 1800s. Four prospectors who struck gold in California buried their profits along the banks of the lake. They stuck a hunting knife in a sturdy pine tree to mark the spot. People say the Indians attacked them swiftly—before they had a chance to leave additional notice of where they'd hidden the gold. Three of the prospectors were killed and the other one ran back East to his home, where they say he died of fright since he had a chance to stop and think about what he'd actually been through. People say the knife is long gone, but the gold is still buried there.

The Grand Lake area has as many stories as it had mines, and the scrappy little towns that sprung up around those mines—including the Ruby and the Wolverine—lived and died by the rumors, tales, and legends that began there. The towns surrounded and sometimes rivaled Grand Lake: There was Teller City, Lulu City, Dutchtown, Gaskill, Crescent City, Manhattan, and the tiny little tent "town" called Hitchen's Camp.

With the help of his dog, Old Man Hitchens ran Hitchen's Gulch at the foot of Red Mountain. When the mutt died, Hitchens got another one that he was equally devoted to. In the course of the old man's life, he had kept company with three dogs. And it was said that his biggest fear was that in death he'd meet them all together in heaven and that each jealous dog would be angry that he wasn't Hitchens' only "best" friend.

After the ore was spent and everybody left camp, Old Man Hitchens continued to run the place with his last dog until he died—Old Man Hitchens, that is. His dog died soon after.

Dutchtown was born of a drunken brawl in nearby Lulu City. Two Dutchmen got drunk, added considerably to the bullet holes in the walls of the saloon, shot up the city in general, and were run out of town. To take care of their hangovers, they staggered a little farther up Red Mountain than was usual; one of them leaned on a pick axe and then wiped the haze away from his eyes long enough to realize that they'd struck it rich. The camp that sprung up there—practically the next day—became known as Dutchtown in their honor.

"Cap'n" Yankee and Ben Franklin Burnett are no doubt still debating from their graves about who founded Lulu City. But if the town name is any indication of who found what first, then Ben Franklin Burnett is the hands-down favorite: Lulu City was named in 1879 for Burnett's daughter. Within a few weeks, the place was swarming with prospectors. Lulu City was quickly plotted out with nineteen streets, one hundred blocks, four sawmills, a hotel, a justice of the peace, and a post office. The town boasted a Saturday-night population of five hundred, including "Squeaky" Bob Wheeler, a character who lived on the outskirts of town at Phantom Valley Ranch.

Squeaky Bob drank a lot, but it didn't affect his strange high-pitched voice, which lent him his nickname. With a few shots of alcohol under his belt, he became known for his gun shots, specifically for shooting up the town. Nevertheless, the man was exceptionally well liked and quite noted for his hospitality. When he wasn't drunk, he charmed his guests, often telling great stories that saved his neck once or twice and kept him out of jail many more times than that.

It took only five years before Squeaky Bob left and the town stood empty. A few miners uncovered some good gold and silver in Lulu City, but the cost of extracting it was too high and most of the ore was too low-grade. It is said that when Lulu City busted in 1884 people left everything they owned—dishes on the table and clothes on the line—and simply pushed on to the next mining town that showed a profit.

A few miles (km) from Lulu, Teller City was at one time the biggest and most important town in the Grand Lake area. Established in 1879, it was named for the "grand old man of Colorado," Senator Henry M. Teller, who had served as secretary of the interior for President Chester A. Arthur.

The population swelled from three hundred to twelve hundred after silver was discovered. One popular hotel in town, the Yates House, boasted forty rooms and a player piano. There were twenty-seven saloons, two sawmills, and a newspaper. But Teller City became best known for the "hundred-foot swindle." A company from the East hired two Teller City men to sink a shaft one hundred feet (30.4 m) deep to look for silver. Well, they dug down fifty feet

Deep in the woods along seldom-used U.S. Forest Service roads, Teller City (opposite, top) stands in ruin. Most of the buildings are remnants, whereas only a century ago a rollicking forty-room hotel served a population of over a thousand. The trail to Lulu City passes the remains of miner Joe Shipler's cabins (opposite, bottom). Once there, however, not one of the nineteen platted streets is visible. There is nothing left of Lulu City to indicate the dreams of five hundred miners who steadfastly stayed on in the snowbound valley during the winter of 1880–81. Only hikers can get to the site, by way of the Colorado River Trail in Rocky Mountain National Park.

Transportation getting to and from Teller City may have been difficult, but it didn't stop the citizenry from horse racing. Past the hotel, the saloons, and the newspaper office, the horses ran, spurred on by heavy bets and eager jockeys. One jockey, who lost by a nose, supposedly kept his horse going, fled into the woods, and ran off with a local parlor girl.

(15 m) in one spot and struck water. They then dug fifty feet in another spot and again struck water. After all was said and done, they had dug a hundred feet, so the two men sent the company a bill for the total, got paid, and left town, never to be heard from again.

A long-standing rivalry between Teller City and Grand Lake came to a head one afternoon along the lake's tragic shores. Making for one of the blackest, bleakest, dingiest chapters in all of Colorado's history, the infamous gunfight that took place there was over politics—more specifically, over the Republican Convention of 1882. John Mills, a lawyer from the then-booming Teller City, was elected a delegate to the state convention. But E. P. Weber, head of Grand Lake's enormously successful Wolverine Mine, and a man named Cap Dean traveled to the convention and contested Mills' election. As a result, the state convention officials seated Dean and Weber instead.

On July 3 of the next year, Weber and another committeeman, Barney Day, held a meeting and "forgot" to invite Mills. The story goes that Mills, who didn't like being ignored and who still insisted that he had a seat at the state convention, gathered together a lynching party to "put a scare" into Dean, Day, and Weber. Acting as friends of Mills and not as officers of the law, Teller City Sheriff Charlie Royer and Undersheriff Billy Redman joined the party.

Dean and his cronies caught wind of the action; with their guns ready and loaded, Dean, Day, and Weber left their meeting at the Grand Lake Hotel and met Mills' band on the banks of the lake.

Shots rang out for a solid afternoon. Hardly anyone in all of Grand Lake ventured outdoors. When all was said and done, neither Day, Dean, Weber, nor Mills ended up getting a seat at the state convention—they all lay dead along the lakeside.

Sheriffs Royer and Redman ran away, but it's debatable whether they escaped retribution. A few weeks after the incident, Royer was found dead from an unlikely "suicide" in a Georgetown hotel room. And some say a man who looked exactly like Redman was found shot along a trail in Utah one month later. Whether their deaths were the work of the vigilantes, friends of Day, Dean, and Weber, or friends of Mills who felt that Royer and Redman had betrayed him, no one knows for sure.

Eagle River Country

There is a mountain in the distant West
That, Sun-defying, in its deep ravines
Displays a cross of snow upon its side.
—Henry Wadsworth Longfellow, *The Cross of Snow*

South and west of Grand Lake, the Eagle River—a tributary of the Colorado—descends by hairpin twists and turns to the floor of Eagle Park, which was once the bed of a prehistoric lake. To the north of this sinuous valley lies an almost forgotten ghost town, Holy Cross City, and beyond that lies the Mount of the Holy Cross, which cannot always be seen.

For years, Indian scouts and frontiersmen told of seeing a giant "cross of snow" mysteriously etched in the mountains. As more and more prospectors arrived in the area, the story grew as fast as a boomtown. The exact location of the cross became a subject of much debate. Some said the cross was cursed because any miner who tried to work the mountain died or met with some horrible tragedy.

In the 1860s, F. V. Hayden and W. H. Jackson, the latter a famous photographer, set out to find the cross and document it. They took many expeditions up into the hills and interviewed perhaps a hundred people before they came across a band of Ute Indians led by Chief Ouray. The Indians knew the location of the cross but did not understand why the white man was so interested in the natural phenomenon.

The Mount of the Holy Cross stands at an altitude of 14,005 feet (4,269 m). A crosslike crevice cuts into the face of the peak measuring 750 feet (229 m) on each horizontal side and 1,500 feet (457 m) along the vertical. The bars of the cross cut roughly 80 feet (24 m) deep into the earth. The cross is most distinctly seen in late spring and early summer when the ravines of the crevices are filled with snow.

Although scarcely known before 1869, once Jackson photographed the peak, it became the

The Mount of the Holy Cross (above) and the land around it were transferred from the Department of Agriculture to the National Park Service soon after it had been made a monument. In 1950, the land reverted to the National Forest Service, and as a result it lost its status as a national monument.

most famous and widely publicized picture of its time. Artists made the long trek up the mountain to paint the cross. Longfellow wrote a poem about it. Then, in 1929, the Mount of the Holy Cross was formally designated a national monument.

The Mount of the Holy Cross was not always the focus of attention in this region where mountains rise up on either side of the Eagle River. At one time, gold was thought to be in those mountains and drew miners to the many towns and camps—among the Battle, French, and Horn mountains—that developed as a result of Leadville's boom to the south. Prospectors soon found the good ore they'd been seeking, and Eagle River became a county in its own right.

Situated north of Eagle River, the mining town of Holy Cross City was named for the Mount of the Holy Cross, which is to the south of the river, but which can't be seen from the town because a mountain range divides the two. Nestled at the foot of Whitney Peak, the town of Holy Cross City had only three hundred people at its peak. A treacherous mountain trail connected the camp with its sister town, Gold Park, which sprang up when an anonymous Frenchman said something about pieces of gold float he'd found in the river. Though small, Holy Cross City had a school, a couple of stores, and some cabins, all of which were deserted by 1883.

In all the folklore of ghost towns of the West, there are hundreds of lost mine and buried treasure stories, but there is not one as extravagant as Eagle River's story of Buck Rogers' lost fortune at Slate Mountain.

In 1849, Rogers—a young prospector—and three fellow miners successfully worked a rich vein they'd discovered in the mountains. They exhausted themselves. The supplies were running low, but there was more gold to be had. So, Rogers left for more provisions. He ended up spending the pooled money, but not on food: The whiskey in town proved to be much too tempting.

Although he'd made short work of going down the mountain, he took his own sweet time getting back up. When he finally returned to the camp, he found everything—his friends, their shack, and all the gold—buried under a deadly cover of snow and dirt. His dalliance saved him from the fatal landslide, but the deaths of his companions changed Rogers forever. He never regained his equanimity; he took to the bottle and was known forever after as a drunk.

Yet the story continues—as lost mine stories tend to do. Thirty-two years later, an old miner walked into a Denver saloon and paid the bartender in gold dust. The old man claimed he had found the treasure of Slate Mountain. "There's plenty more where that dust came from," he told the bartender. He also told the barkeep, however, that he'd had to kill his partner, because he'd gotten a little too greedy when it came time to divide the money.

After a few more drinks, the old man got down to the details. He'd strangled his unfortunate partner, the miner said, and buried the body at Brush Creek. In a drunken stupor, the prospector handed the directions to Slate Mountain to the patient bartender. The miner then left the saloon and was never heard from again. But that's not where it ends, either.

Not long after his encounter with the miner, the bartender got so sick he was not able to look for Slate Mountain himself. His illness worsened, forcing him to seek out the help of a doctor. The bartender had little money and fewer possessions, but the doctor had heard of the miner's story and asked for the directions in lieu of cash.

Go along Eagle River to the mouth of Brush Creek, follow creek five miles (8 km) to the forks. Take east branch coming almost to water's edge. Follow dry gulch running north until you come to four large trees standing close together with the bark all taken off. About two feet (.61 m) around it, turn due east and go directly up hill until you come to small hole dug in the ground. Continue on until you come to another hole, and so on, until you come to the third hole. This line is also marked by blazed trees on both sides. From the third hole turn due north and about two hundred feet (60.9 m) from the last blazed tree you will see three tall trees standing in a triangle. The trees have their tops broken off about thirty feet (9 m) up. This is about three hundred feet (91 m) from the timberline, and the vein runs north and south on the place described.

The doctor went in search of the gold but, even with the barkeep's directions, was never able to find the spot.

The search was renewed in 1892 by Arthur H. Fulford, the former marshal of Redcliff, one of the largest camps in the area and Eagle River's county seat. He managed to find a partner fool enough to go with him up the moun-

Holy Cross City lies at the end of a well-maintained but treacherous (for jeeps) jeep trail, high in the Holy Cross Wilderness outside of Redcliff. Little remains to be seen of the town, although the mining area a bit farther up the path offers many rewards, including this mine entrance (left).

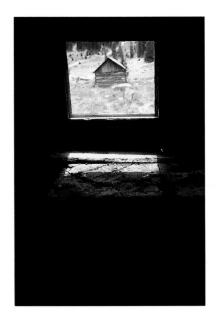

Like most unpreserved ghost towns, the cabins and mining debris are left for future generations on an honor system. The National Forest Service oversees the remaining structures and equipment (above), but visitors should abide by the law of taking photographs and nothing else.

tain, but before they left, the partner was mysteriously killed in a barroom fight. Fulford set out himself and was killed by a snowslide on New Year's Day. His body—and the gold—were never found.

Another memorable story to come out of Eagle River focuses on an old ranch house that doubled as a hideout for one of the west's most notorious outlaws and escape artists, Harry Tracy. Born Harry Severn about 1875 somewhere in Kentucky, Harry Tracy had a miserable childhood. His mother died when he was young, and his father, a livery stable worker, ignored him. At sixteen, Harry robbed his hometown post office and killed the sheriff. Thus began his notorious life as an arrogant fugitive. Leaving a childhood sweetheart, Genie Carter, in Kentucky, Tracy headed for Colorado's gold camps, where his square jaw and icy blue eyes gained him the attention of other ladies.

The handsome youth found no gold in Colorado, however, so he moved on. He worked as a cowpuncher in Montana, as a fireman for the Northern Pacific Railroad in Seattle, and then returned to Colorado to run the chuck-a-luck and roulette tables in Cripple Creek. From town to town, he killed people wherever he went.

He hadn't forgotten Genie Carter, however, and once he was settled in Cripple Creek, he sent for her. For a while they lived peacefully together in a boardinghouse until an ex-marshall of Leadville made a vulgar remark to Genie and Tracy challenged the man to a "fast-draw" in the street. Tracy killed him fair and square, and afterward turned himself in at the sheriff's office. When Carter came to see him, she slipped him a gun, and the pair escaped to Utah. Tracy was soon arrested and sentenced to seven years for robbing a mule train of ten thousand dollars in gold. Carter had been his accomplice, but she somehow avoided capture.

"I'll die before I let them put me behind bars," Tracy is reported to have said many times over. So it seemed only natural that he escaped from Utah State Prison, where he planned the first of his many Houdini-like escapes. During his sixty-day stay in the prison, Tracy carved a wooden pistol out of a chunk of pine. While the other prisoners were digging ditches in the yard, Tracy put the "pistol" to a guard's head. Tracy, along with his new-found partners, Tom Lent and Jack Bennett, took the guard's weapons. The outlaw Tracy dressed in the guard's clothes and escorted his three "prisoners" out of the yard.

The trio split outside the wall with Tracy and Lent beating a path of terror into Colorado. Lawmen from Utah, Wyoming, and Colorado chased Tracy and Lent into the Brown's Hole region of northwestern Colorado. After a lengthy confrontation, one member of the posse was dead and Tracy and Lent were recaptured. Tracy was taken to Hahn's Peak Jail but escaped. He was recaptured and jailed again. Security was so tight that there was no possible chance of escape, so Tracy and Lent cooked up a plan whereby they slept during the day and made such noise and commotion at night that they were soon transferred to Aspen's Pitkin County Jail. After the transfer, Tracy escaped again by attacking a guard with an iron post from his bed frame. Lent disappeared into legend, while Tracy went on to menace every state in the Northwest.

He and his sweetheart reunited and eventually set up a ranch in Idaho. Suspecting Tracy of cattle rustling, vigilantes stormed the place, inadvertently killing Carter in the shoot-out. Tracy fled but was arrested and jailed again in Oregon, where the authorities placed him in the "Oregon Boot," a twenty-five-pound (9.3 kg) iron shoe that was locked or welded around a prisoner's ankle. Tracy escaped yet again and became the object of the largest manhunt in the history of the West.

Tracy eluded his pursuers several times. He even continued to commit crimes while on the run until a young attorney, Maurice Smith, organized a posse that caught up with the outlaw on a ranch near Creston, Washington. Tracy's gun sight was knocked out of line in the course of the shoot-out, causing the crack shot to repeatedly miss his targets. Smith shot Tracy in the leg. Bleeding profusely, Tracy decided to take his own life rather than face another day in jail. He shot himself just above his right eye at sundown on August 3, 1902.

Creede

Creede is unfortunate in getting more of the flotsam of the state than usually falls to the lot of mining camps . . . some of her citizens would take sweepstake prizes at a hog show.
—from the *Creede Candle*, April 29, 1892

Located in the southwestern part of Colorado, Creede lies northeast of Antler's Park, a glimmer of the once-boisterous mining town that sat perched on stilts and high foundations over the rapid waters of the Rio Grande. The seat of Mineral County, Creede sits at the base of a dramatic and astonishingly beautiful gorge. Creede led the district in silver production during the silver bonanza of the 1890s,

The Holy Moses (below) was the mine that started it all in Creede. The rush began in 1890, and by 1892, eight thousand (some say ten thousand) people had come to Creede. Accommodations were so tight that the railroad, which had arrived the year before, allowed the homeless to sleep in its parked Pullman cars.

thanks to the Holy Moses, Amethyst, and King Solomon mines. Gambling and business were conducted all day and all night. The old mills ran turbines that supplied the town's single street with electricity twenty-four hours a day.

The rush started in 1890 when silver was discovered at the Holy Moses Mine. N. C. Creede was taking a break for lunch when he slammed his pick axe into the ground and hit pay dirt. "Holy Moses," he is reported to have said, "I've struck it rich." Six million dollars' worth of silver was taken out of the hills around Creede within the year, but N. C. Creede was never able to enjoy his good fortune. He died in Los Angeles in 1897, broke and unhappy. They say he committed suicide by morphine. As a newspaper of the day, the *Apex Pine Cone*, reported, Creede had separated from his wife, she "wanted to live with him again, and he preferred death."

Creede came into being in 1891 and within a few short months overran many of the surrounding camps. Real estate was at a premium. There were claim jumpers and lot jumpers alike. The unwritten rule was that if you claimed a lot you had to start building that day. If you didn't, you lost the claim by the time the sun went down. Houses were often built, bought, and sold within a week for thousands of dollars.

But what made Creede especially interesting were its characters. The town housed perhaps the most diverse group of citizens ever to come together in one place. There were Bible-

Creede today is a lively little town whose elevation far exceeds its population: 362 people live tucked into the base of a dramatic gorge at 8,852 feet (2,798 m) above sea level. Just above the gorge, on a dirt "loop" road, lies Bachelor, a true ghost of a town that flourished at the turn of the century. To get to Bachelor, explorers must pass Willow Creek Canyon (opposite left) and the Commodore Mine (opposite right and above). Almost two hundred miles of tunnels run through Bachelor Mountain, the site of the Commodore mine.

pounders, merchants, mining tycoons, prospectors, and a colorful cross section of underworld rogues. Staggering from gulch to gambling hall, whorehouse to church sermon, ten thousand men and women descended on Creede during its first few months of existence. Among them was a gangster by the name of Bob Ford, who is said to have waltzed into town, opened up the Exchange Saloon, and told everybody he was running things. He didn't get many arguments: Ford had gunned down "Mr. Howard" (alias Jesse James).

Ford's antics got so out of hand, however, that the town was forced to organize a vigilante committee and elect a mayor. The vigilante committee's first job was to run Ford out of town. The saloon owner left but asked the vigilante committee if he could return for a day to close out his business. Ford came back to Creede, but instead of closing his business, he built another saloon, Ford's Saloon.

On the eve of opening the new place, June 10, 1892, which was shortly after one of the two fires that almost destroyed Creede, Ford was promptly shot and killed by a man named Ed O'Kelly. Some say O'Kelly shot him because of a gambling debt; others say it was because Ford had harassed O'Kelly's parents; and still others believe that it was because Ford had "gunned down Mr. Howard" and O'Kelly was married to a sister of a member in Jesse James' gang (one of the Younger brothers) and O'Kelly didn't like the idea of Jesse being dead.

Sleepless Creede

Here's a land where all are equal—
   Of high and lowly birth—
A land where men make millions,
   Dug from the dreary earth.
Here meek and mild-eyed burros
   On mineral mountains feed.
It's day all day in the daytime
   And there is no night in Creede.
The cliffs are solid silver
   With wondrous wealth untold,
And the beds of the running rivers
   Are lined with the purest gold.
While the world is filled with sorrow,
   And hearts must break and
   bleed—
It's day all day in the daytime,
   And there is no night in Creede.
                              —Cy Warman

The area around Creede is pocked with mines (opposite), many of which are still active.

Everyone rejoiced upon hearing of Ford's death, but the vigilante committee almost lynched O'Kelly for not obeying their authority. O'Kelly served a short prison term at Canon City but not before attending Ford's funeral—a party that lasted for days with much dancing on the dead man's grave.

A hustler who ran a two-bit con game on the streets of Creede, Soapy Smith, had lorded over the rough element in town even before Ford was killed. Soapy got his name from a ruse he worked from camp to camp that never failed. He sold soap on street corners, and in front of his customers he'd wrap the bars in paper, slipping a one, two, five, ten, twenty, or one hundred dollar bill underneath the plain wrapping. Or so it appeared. With sleight of hand, he controlled the game, and only his shills walked away with the higher denominations. Bars sold for five dollars to twenty-five dollars, and Soapy had his finger in every dirty pie in Creede until he moved his business up to the Klondike.

Men by no means had a monopoly on corruption in Creede. "Poker" Alice, an Amazon-like cardsharp who frequented a number of towns in the West, was known to relieve many a prospector of his diggings over a quick game of straight poker. "Killarney" Kate, another one of Creede's wildcats, was notorious for gambling and cigar smoking.

Lillie Lovell and Rose Vastine were also characters—in addition to being the town's top

madams. On February 3, 1893, the *Creede Candle* reported that the six-foot-two Rose Vastine, known as "Timberline," tried to commit suicide by pumping herself full of lead when she "became weary of the trials and tribulations of this wicked world and decided to take a trip over the range, and to this end brought into play a forty-one calibre pistol. With the muzzle at her lily-white breast and her index finger on the trigger she waited not to contemplate the sad result." Timberline shot six bullets into her chest, some of which went through her left lung, and she still survived.

The *Candle* also reported (September 15, 1893) the story of Lulu Slain, a drug addict who "laid aside the camellia for the poppy and passed into the beyond early Wednesday morning. She and the Mormon Queen (a fellow drug addict) had been living in a small cabin in upper Creede but the times grew hard and the means of life came not. They sought relief from life with morphine, the inevitable end of their unfortunate kind, a well-trodden path from Creede. Lulu's dead; the Queen lives."

Cy Warman, "the poet of Cochitopa," was Creede's most legitimate native son. Warman came to Colorado in 1880 because he was fascinated with railroads. He worked for many years on the Denver & Rio Grande Railroad before moving to Creede. He was a poet who became a journalist, an editor for the *Creede Candle*, and, later, an editor for the New York *Sun*.

Today, Creede boasts a population of 362, and its characters are still its best asset.

Lake City

The mountain tops are clothed in white,
The old prospector still gets tight,
The burrow winds around the hill,
A carrying ores to Crooke's big mill.
—from "Hang Him"
published in Lake City's *Silver World*

All roads led to Lake City, the hub of a mining district, connecting it with the smaller, surrounding mining camps and the beautiful San Cristobal Lake. One of the busiest cities in its boom years, Lake City always had its share of trouble. There was even a big Indian battle as late as 1879, but what Lake City is most remembered for today is a little more unusual.

It was the first place in the United States where a man was tried for the crime of cannibalism.

Cannibalism never reached large proportions in the West, but the fact that it happened and was sometimes necessary to survive was well known. Everyone had heard about the deliciously scandalous trials of the Donner Party, who, in an unsuccessful bid to stay alive, resorted to cannibalism in the treacherous, snow-capped mountains of the Sierra Nevada. Somewhere there was an unwritten rule that if ever a person was put in a life-or-death situation such as the Donner Party's, he or she could not eat a relative. A stranger, however, was acceptable.

During a particularly trying expedition into the Colorado Rockies in 1848, John Fremont, a government explorer who gained fame investigating the Oregon territory, sent ahead four scouts who almost perished. One did die; by the time Fremont could reach the party, the surviving three had finished off the unfortunate one.

Writers Horace Greeley and Henry Villard traveled around Colorado and wrote about the rumors of cannibalism during the Pike's Peak Rush in 1859: HORRIBLE FROM THE PLAINS ran the headline of the New York *Tribune* on May 28, 1859. STARVATION AND CANNIBALISM appeared in slightly smaller type. The telegraphed report told of a stage agent who picked up a "man named Blue, who was reduced to a skeleton from starvation. He had started with his two brothers. One of them died, and the remaining two ate his body." It related another story, then goes on to say that not one or two but "about five hundred returning emigrants . . . confirm the previous accounts of the suffering and privations on the plain."

Another report came from a well-known, early Denver character known as "Old Phil the Cannibal" who used to boast about the men he ate. According to Old Phil, the heads, hands, and feet were tasty and had the flavor of pork, but the rest of the body was tough and difficult to digest.

The famous western scout, John "Liver-eating" Johnston, was notorious for killing and scalping Indians and then eating their livers. A mass murderer of his day, he supposedly butchered more than three hundred Crow Indians. Johnston denied the charges but couldn't stop people from saying, "Watch out, or Liver-eating Johnston'll get you."

It is now believed that these and other stories were becoming so common that something had to be done about it. Many think Al Packer, "the Lake City Cannibal," was made an example in an attempt to stop the stories.

In December 1873, Packer led a party of prospectors from Utah up into the San Juan Mountains to look for gold. They reached the camp of the Ute chief, Ouray, who advised the group to stay put until the spring when the traveling would be less hazardous. Most of the party agreed, but six men—Packer, Bell, Humphreys, Swan, Noon, and Miller—decided

to continue. Six weeks later, Packer appeared alone at the Los Pinos Agency, seventy-five miles (120 km) from Lake City. Packer claimed the others in his party abandoned him when he became lame, and he was left to eat roots and bark.

The problem was no one believed him. Packer appeared to be fine and asked the people at the agency for whiskey first, not food. Packer also said he had no money, but he appeared days later in nearby Saguache drinking and gambling. Meanwhile, an Indian scout found strips of human flesh and bone along Packer's route and suspicions flared. *Harper's Weekly* published photos of the cannibalized bodies and crushed skulls of five men found near Slumgullion Pass.

Packer claimed that starvation drove his partners mad and that he had to kill Bell in self-defense. Then he discovered that Bell had

Today, tourism accounts for much of Lake City's vitality, but in the 1870s, lead and silver mining brought prosperity to the miners who prospected on what was then Ute Indian land. An 1873 treaty moved the Utes south to the plains, and pioneers spilled into the new town, just four miles from placid Lake San Cristobal (opposite). The McClelland-Abston House (above) is a fine example of a typical rooming house from the mid-1870s.

Visitors are welcome to stroll through the Lake City Courthouse (right, top and bottom) except when court is in session. An exhibit of Al Packer (below) memorabilia hangs in the first-floor hall; in the courtroom on the second floor, the District Court Record lies under glass open to the page inscribed "11th day, April Term 1883, April 13th, '83, The People of the State of Colorado vs Alfred Packer."

killed the rest of his party. Packer was arrested, but there were no prisons at the Los Pinos Agency, so they chained Packer to a rock. He escaped but was recaptured in Wyoming in 1883 and brought to Lake City where he was tried for murder and sentenced to hang.

testify that maybe the people would kind of shrink from me after all the things that have been said, but there was nothing of the kind. They seemed like they wanted to see me." The authorities let Packer visit the theater when he was in Denver. He said, "And what I liked

As the story goes, the Lake City judge who tried Packer was a Democrat. When he sentenced Packer, he supposedly yelled, "You so and so, there were seven Democrats in Hinsdale County and you ate five of them. . . . I sentence you to be hanged by the neck until you are dead, dead, dead."

Packer was sentenced but not to death. He got off on a technicality and received forty years for manslaughter. During his jail term, Packer was brought to Denver to testify in another case. He told a reporter: "I thought when I was told about having to come to Denver and

about it most was that it wasn't anything vulgar. . . . There was skirt dancing in it, and all that, but not one of those girls lifted her feet higher than that [Packer indicated about a foot and a half (.46 m) above the ground]."

Packer served a lot of his term, but then a woman from Denver, Polly Pry, who was sympathetic to Packer's situation, got the case reopened and won Packer's release. Packer became a doorman for the *Denver Post* and worked there until he died in 1907. Not long afterward, a marker was placed in Slumgullion Pass.

When the bank building on the busiest corner of town (left) was completed in August 1877, few would have believed it would some day be a hotel or a post office that showed silent movies and sold candy. It was the pride of its day, constructed with a solid stone masonry vault and a safe that weighed five thousand pounds (2,267.9 kg). All the safeguards, however, did not prevent the bank's first president from embezzling over forty thousand dollars in cash.

South Pass City

Damned fools and their scalps are soon parted.
—Jim Bridger, frontier scout

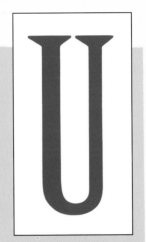

Until the early 1820s, trappers and frontiersmen got along well with the many Indian tribes thriving in and around this long, low, and gentle pass that crosses the Wind River Range some 7,500 feet (2,286 m) above sea level. The Bannock, Ute, Arapaho, Snake, Sioux, and Crow Indians all hunted and camped in the area along the nearby clear creek known as the Sweetwater. Then the missionaries came, bringing with them their brides, their Bibles, and their own way of looking at the world. And the miners followed: They muddied the drinking water, killed off the food supply, and violated the earth. Missionaries, miners, pioneers—each group carved out tracks that ultimately became the Pony Express, the Oregon, Mormon, California, and Overland trails, oxen-driven cuts that cut even deeper into the Indians' way of life. The pioneers' wagons and stages zigzagged across sacred Indian camps and burial grounds, tearing up traditions as the vehicles rent the land.

The South Pass Mail Road climbs the southeastern slopes of the range, cutting a long, narrow shelf before it drops into hillsides scabbed with prospect holes and rot-

South Pass City State Historic Site (opposite and inset) is a rewarding, off-the-beaten-path tourist attraction.

Although men mined gold in South Pass intermittently from 1842 on, the goldfields didn't really develop until about two decades later when a detachment of soldiers on the trail of horse thieves stopped to pan in Willow Creek. These enlisted men tried their luck wherever they camped. Here at South Pass, they recovered enough gold to induce them to return in the fall of 1866. By May of 1868, one gold rusher wrote, "This should have been named the City of Rumors. . . . Every day there is a new report and excitement about 'placers.' . . ." Everyone wanted to "make the riffle," or strike it rich; few did, yet approximately six million dollars was taken out of the earth around South Pass City (opposite, top). Visitors coming to see the well-preserved buildings now usually enter the town by crossing the footbridge (opposite, bottom).

ting sluice boxes. The road winds through Atlantic City and climbs again into the hills to a barren summit, one of the oldest mining areas in the state, South Pass City.

Although it's not set in stone, many historians believe that General William Ashley of the Rocky Mountain Fur Company was the first white man to "discover" the pass. A colleague, General Henry Atkinson, reported Ashley's findings in 1824 when he wrote "there is an easy passage . . . indeed so gentle as to admit wagons to be taken over." In the 1830s, missionaries Henry Spalding and Marcus Whitman traveled through the pass on their way to Oregon to convert the Indians. Their wives, Narcissa Prentice Whitman and Eliza Hart Spalding, were the first white women to cross the path. "Is it a reality or a dream," wrote Mrs. Spalding in her journal on July 4, 1836, "that after four months of painful journeying I am alive and actually standing at the summit of the Rocky Mountains where the foot of white woman has never before trod?" Mrs. Spalding was pregnant and in pain for most of her grueling journey. The Whitman-Spalding marker still stands on the west slope of the pass where the party paused near Pacific Springs.

But it wasn't until 1842 when a party of miners returning East from California sank a shaft in the Sweetwater Creek and found gold that life in South Pass became earmarked for permanent and profound change. Prospectors panned for gold like birds building a nest in a

cat house. The risk of being scalped was high and mining progress slow. The Indians, who by this time hated the settlers and looked on them as intruders, watched and waited in the hills for the best time to attack. Miners going to and from their diggings for supplies were often ambushed and killed.

Supply-wagon drivers were especially vulnerable. Billy Rhodes was one, and he was found by the trailside scalped. Another freighter known as "Uncle Ben" was able to repulse an attack on his supply wagon and come out of the scuffle on his feet, although his driver fell. The man was hurt but alive. Uncle Ben, wounded himself, left his gun and ammunition with the driver, and tied the wounded man to the bottom of the wagon, wrapping him in blankets for protection and piling rocks around him for camouflage. Thinking his partner safe, Ben went to round up a posse. He returned, but the Indians had also returned, finished off his friend, and taken the supplies. The posse was attacked on its way back to South Pass City, sending the men scattering for cover among the willows. One member of the posse tried to race back to town for more help but was shot through the head. Later on, an even larger posse assembled to chase the Indians, but they were unable to track them down. Not a white soul felt safe in South Pass City.

However, the miners' vision of developing Sweetwater into gold heaven was too great. They persisted and eventually got the government to send experienced Indian fighters, such

as Jim Bridger and Jim Baker, to accompany the men to the mines. Soon Fort Stambaugh was erected nearby. Lieutenant Colonel J. W. Anthony was authorized by the governor to gather companies of volunteers to fight the Indians. He had no trouble finding recruits but was then instructed to wage his campaign against the Indians without killing them. The lieutenant colonel promptly refused the commission, and the enlightened man who gave the instructions is forgotten.

On November 11, 1865, South Pass City was officially established as the first mining district of the Wyoming organization. Although the Dakota territory recognized the South Pass region

*O*ne store (above) remains open at South Pass City. Reminiscent of the old days, it sells stick candy and licorice. Inside, history buffs will also find South Pass 1868, a journal of the Wyoming gold rush, and other personal recollections of the South Pass area.

as a part of their Carter County, most of the people living in the region disregarded the connection. As one old-timer put it, "We didn't know the laws of Dakota, and we paid no attention to them. We got along this way very well." Despite repeated problems with claim jumpers and the continuing Indian menace, mine sites like the Carissa, Carrie Shields, Young America, and Mohamet flourished.

There were times in South Pass when citizens weren't sure which was worse, being scalped by Indians or being shot by outlaws. It was often said that the deeds of one outlaw called "Mountain Jack" Alvese far outdid anything perpetrated on the miners and townspeople by the Indians. After deserting General Albert Johnston's army (which was headed for Utah to put down the Mormons), Mountain Jack hid out with the Shoshone Indians. To disguise himself, he dressed like a Shoshone and lived among them as their adopted brother. While the Shoshone were generally friendly, Mountain Jack had other plans. Using the Shoshone teepees as a base, Mountain Jack robbed trains, plundered stagecoaches, pounced on supply wagons, and showed no compunction at all about killing men, women, or children. From 1857 on, he terrorized the region, leaving only once to test the rough waters of Virginia City. The vigilantes there, however, pushed him back to South Pass, and he returned to live with the Shoshone.

Judge William Carter called Mountain Jack's method of hijacking the "forced loan" because at the point of a six-gun, hizzoner was once forced to "loan" Mountain Jack five hundred dollars.

Almost ten years after Mountain Jack moved into the area, the judge saw his nemesis's demise. That winter, Mountain Jack Alvese met his match and shortly after that his maker. Two traders, Johnson and Jackson, brought a load of goods up to the Popo Agie, a summit in the Wind River range, to trade with the Indians. They set up quarters at a roadside camp called Three Cabins. At Three Cabins, Mountain Jack robbed Johnson and Jackson of several thousand dollars' worth of goods and retreated to the Shoshone teepees.

He promptly lost the goods gambling with his Shoshone brothers and returned to Three Cabins in a sour mood. Mountain Jack somehow got it in his head that Johnson had reported his thievery to the Montana vigilantes. Johnson's fellow trader overheard Mountain Jack saying he was going to kill Johnson. It was a cold night when Mountain Jack sat inside one of Three Cabins' cabins wrapped in a huge buffalo robe with a long gun across his lap. Johnson's friend, Jackson, put a rifle by the cabin entrance and told Johnson, who was headed for the cabin, that "Mountain Jack is laying for you inside." Johnson, fed up with Mountain Jack, strode inside. Mountain Jack went for his gun, but before he could get a shot off, Johnson gunned his would-be attacker down. "He was a desperate character," wrote one resident in a letter, "and we are glad to be rid of him."

While Mountain Jack Alvese was South Pass City's most feared character, Esther McQuigg Morris, who later became known as "the mother of women's suffrage in Wyoming," was the city's most renowned. One of the first women ever to take a stand for equal rights, Esther Morris continued her fight once she arrived at South Pass City.

She was orphaned at eleven years old, probably in Illinois, where she later married Artemis Slack, a wealthy railroad contractor. Morris had acquired a small fortune as a businesswoman; when her husband died, she fought for but lost her claims as a widow due to unjust property laws of the state. After that experience, Esther McQuigg spoke out for women's rights with even greater strength. She went on to marry a merchant named John Morris and moved to South Pass City. It was here that Esther Morris supposedly held a tea party that gained her fame not as a historic figure but as a legend.

Story goes that she invited voters and the two candidates who were then running for election to the legislature—William H. Bright and Captain H. Nickerson. At the tea party, Ms. Morris supposedly finagled a promise from each candidate that in the event that he won the election he would introduce a bill giving equal rights to women. William Bright won the election and, according to the legend, true to his word, introduced the bill for women's rights. Yet Todd Guenther says the tea party never took place, and as historian and curator

of the restored ghost town of South Pass City, he should know.

He explained that Wyoming became a full territory in 1869 and its first legislature was about to convene in Cheyenne. Guenther said that Esther Morris did not meet Bright until after the election, and she did not, as many believe, co-author the women's suffrage bill. So much for "history."

In that same year, however, Esther Morris was elected the first female justice of the peace in the United States. She was a great motherly woman with good common sense and a good sense of humor. One of her first cases was against her predecessor James Stillman, who

In 1870, W.H. Jackson photographed South Pass City from this point (above), which is marked on a low hillside just outside of town. Jackson also participated in the expedition to Mount of the Holy Cross in Colorado (see page 63). His photographs, and the documentation of other professionals like him, helped open up the West.

Miner's Delight (above) lies just over the hills from Atlantic City. Jonathan Pugh eventually moved to Atlantic and gained a reputation for telling the saloon owner to "turn her loose." An evening like that, where Pugh paid for everyone in the house, probably cost him over twelve hundred dollars.

refused to pass the court docket on to a woman. Of this incident Morris said:

I went to call on him, and found his wife ill, his twin sons crying and everything in disorder. Judge Stillman was in a foul mood. Besides his having been ousted by a woman, his household was in a distraught state. I had twin sons and knew something of what the trouble was. I stayed and took care of his children and wife, and we became good friends.

Morris dismissed the case on February 14, 1870, and starting her own new docket, began presiding over cases. In the beginning of her term, some people in town tried to force her to leave office, but her decisions were fair and her rule stern, a combination that changed the opinions of those who had rallied against her. Morris heard thirty-four cases, among them ones dealing with assault and battery and intent to kill.

Of her experiences as justice of the peace she said, "Mine was a test of woman's ability to hold office and during it all I do not know that I have neglected my family any more than in ordinary shopping."

Full of danger and profit during the late 1860s, by the late 1870s when the ore started to peter out, South Pass City became full of dust and empty spaces instead. The Union Pacific made its way into Wyoming but never quite made it to South Pass City. With Indian trouble a distant and long-forgotten memory, the Sweetwater Creek now winds its way through pockmarked ravines and scabbed gulches, and South Pass City, where hundreds of desperate but hopeful prospectors once panned for gold, stands restored, welcoming a new breed of prospectors: tourists.

Miner's Delight

I was always glad I never made a strike, for it seemed those who did, their wealth never did them any good. The men who discovered Miner's Delight—Jonathan Pugh drank himself to death; McGovern killed a man, went to the pen and when he got out was in another scrape, got stabbed and killed—when any of them got rich, they didn't know what to do with it.
—J. E. Anoston, former resident of Miner's Delight

In the cemetery of Miner's Delight, markers indicated the grave of two women (one is J. E. Anoston's mother) and several men who were massacred in 1868 by Sioux Indians. The graves remained unmarked for fifty-six years until the young Anoston, who survived the attack, returned to the site to pay tribute to his mother's death.

The Anostons followed the old Oregon Trail in 1868, believing the stories they heard about a better way of life, about finding gold, growing rich, and living happily ever after. What they found instead were hard times and tragedy.

Located in the southwestern part of Wyoming, the early settlement of Miner's Delight sprang up within a seven-mile radius of the

Wind, Sweetwater, and Green rivers. One of South Pass' rowdiest satellite "cities," the tiny tent town sat atop Peabody Hill about four miles from Atlantic City and overlooked Spring Creek as it flowed into Wind River.

Jonathan Pugh first struck gold in 1867 when he walked out of his cabin one morning and saw gold flecks in Spring Creek reflecting in the sunlight. Pugh staked the claim in his own name and in the name of his partners, Frank McGovern and Jack Holbrook. By the fall of 1869, prospectors flooded the area and Miner's Delight was born. Pugh hired an experienced miner named George McKay from California to oversee one of their mills. He brought in pickers and sluicers and the camp grew. The ore was plentiful, with values sometimes running as high as thousands of dollars to the ton. More mills were built to speed up the rewards, and in one six-month period, the yield came to three hundred thousand dollars.

Some pulled up stakes once they struck it rich. The Cheyenne *Leader* of December 11, 1868, reported that Judge Dildine and Dave Mason left town to "go East to enjoy the fruits of their good fortune and hard work." But most people stayed in Miner's Delight. In its heyday, the town boomed to a population of two thousand. Other towns in the area, like Atlantic City and South Pass, held church meetings in their hotel lobbies. Miner's Delight put on no such airs. There were several saloons, whorehouses, and faro joints. Miners won and lost fortunes on a Saturday night. It was a riproaring gold-mining town with a reputation for letting "'er run wide open."

The most widely known woman in Wyoming, "Calamity" Jane, drank all night and

A typical U.S. Geological Survey report from the early mining days comes from Miner's Delight: "The Miner's Delight mill has ten stamps, and is driven by a 40-horse-power engine, which uses two and one half cords of wood per day. The stamps weigh 425 pounds each, and crush from 10 to 12 tons of ore per 24 hours. They are geared to fall 14 inches, at the rate of from 40 to 70 drops per minute; 70 for hard and 40 for decomposed quartz. The tailings are very rich in both gold and quicksilver." A few cabins (above and left), also typical of their day, are all that's left of Miner's Delight.

raised hell all day in Miner's Delight. She was orphaned at nearby Fort Bridger in 1868 and learned many of her skills as a gunfighter in the boomtown. As one historian, Alfred Mokler, wrote: "When Miner's Delight was a prosperous but wild gold-mining town in the '60s, Mary Jane Canary was a poor, neglected little girl who did not know right from wrong, and whose associates were the rough men of that rough country." Mary Jane eventually left Wyoming for New York City to learn to be "educated and civilized."

There she became quite a sensation, putting on shooting exhibitions in her buckskins, making money, and cavorting like hell. When she returned to Miner's Delight, her new-found "education" caused a scandal. Respectable people whispered that "Jane's light of decency had gone out." She eventually left the pass to become an Indian scout, but the town of Miner's Delight most certainly influenced her roaming and restless nature thereafter.

In a town where winter brought blizzards and snowdrifts hundreds of feet (m) high and oppressive Indian raids accompanied the summer, another woman, Mrs. Margaret Burke Heenan, overcame unbeatable odds. Her husband was ambushed and scalped while hauling hay, an incident that triggered widespread outrage throughout the region and several pleas to the government for protection. A letter printed in the Cheyenne *Leader* on September 10, 1872, read:

Yesterday the Indians made a raid on this place, killing a man by the name of Mike Heenan, one of our esteemed citizens, and took the four mules he was driving. About sixty Indians made their appearance in sight of Camp Stambaugh . . . so they have again cleaned the country of all the stock. . . . I hear the peace commissioners are on the road to treat with the Indians, and I suppose they are armed with Quaker applesauce. . . . Respectfully, H.A.N.

After the slaying, Mrs. Heenan took her three small children to a log house and opened up a boardinghouse. Her tenants paid her in nuggets and gold dust, which she saved in a pickle jar. With her first one hundred dollars, she bought a cow and then another and another, until she had enough cows to round up. The first woman ever to run a cattle herd, Margaret Burke Heenan started the Circle H Ranch, named in honor of her late husband.

High on the Continental Divide, Battle (opposite, top) was once so big that it boasted four general stores. Now, nothing remains. Standing nearby on the side of the road is a relatively modern shack (opposite, below).

Battle

*The sawmill in Battle right in town furnishes
the best music—the music of industry.*
—from a Denver newspaper, 1899

Once tucked in among the mountains and
timber of the Sierra Madre just west of the Continental Divide, the town of Battle got its name
from the many skirmishes that took place
there. Frontiersman Jim Baker and a party of
men found themselves surrounded by Arapaho
and Ute at the juncture of Battle Creek and Little Snake rivers. They dug pits to protect themselves and fought off the Indians for two days.
The Indians eventually tired and left without
killing anyone. In another instance, a man
named Henry Fraeb and four members of the
Rocky Mountain Fur Company were killed by
Indians there in 1841.

But Battle is most remembered for the often deadly rivalry between its sheepherders
and cattlemen. The Indians hated the miners,
the miners hated the cattlemen, the cattlemen
hated the sheepherders, and the sheepherders
hated the Mexicans. Everybody hated everybody else, and the graveyards did a booming
business.

Battle's herders had a particularly hard
time with the town's miners. When the first
copper lode was discovered in 1879, a camp
sprang up that quickly became an overnight
stop for gamblers and gunmen, prospectors
and freighters. Unfortunately, the profitable

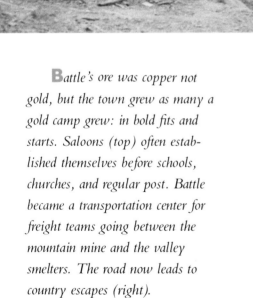

Battle's ore was copper not gold, but the town grew as many a gold camp grew: in bold fits and starts. Saloons (top) often established themselves before schools, churches, and regular post. Battle became a transportation center for freight teams going between the mountain mine and the valley smelters. The road now leads to country escapes (right).

Rudefeha Mine and the Doane Rambler sat right on top of the shepherds' prime grazing land. According to the tales that get passed down from one generation to the next, one night a group of herders stopped in for a drink at a saloon and started an argument with the notorious gambler and crack shot, "Kid" Blizzard. Armed with a whiskey bottle, Kid Blizzard hit a herder on top of his head, and before you could say lamb stew, the entire place broke out in a melee. Kid Blizzard took a shot in the heel but survived. The nameless herder didn't fare well. He was found dead behind the school-house the next morning.

Guns were needed in Battle for protection against these warring factions. It was the kind of town where if a resident came upon a miner shot through the head lying dead on the road-side, he'd silently pass by and no one would ever hear anything more about it. Kid Blizzard went on to kill two Mexicans at Smyzer's Bar for looking at him the wrong way. Everyone knew the Kid killed them, but no one did any-thing about it. At the inquest, the Mexicans were said to have died "from causes unknown."

During the Spanish-American War, the de-mand for copper increased and the town did its best business. Battle had five saloons; a news-paper; two competing hotels, run by Otto Dahl and Mrs. Kinsella, respectively, that shared a rivalry sometimes resembling the one between the sheepherders and miners; an assay office; a false-fronted town hall where people often gathered to complain about the herders; and a whorehouse called Paste-faced Camille's. Battle was on the cutting edge.

Like so many towns in the West, once the mines played out, Battle turned ghost. A marker, put up by the Forest Service among the ruins of Battle years ago, was all that remained for many years: Town site of Battle. Established 1898. Abandoned 1907.

Tubb Town

We're Buzzards from the Barrens, on a tear;
    Hear us toot!
We're the Rockers from the Rockies
    On the shoot!
Saturday nights we hit the town
    Paint it red!
Choke the sheriff, turn the marshall upside down
    On his head!
Call for drinks for all the party
And if chinned by any smarty
    Pay in lead!
                  —old cowboy ballad

Tubb Town sits in the middle of Sioux coun-try, just south of the Black Hills in the north-eastern corner of Wyoming by the South Dakota border. In a treaty signed in 1868 at Fort Laramie, the government "gave" the Black Hills territory to the Sioux and their leaders Red Cloud, Crazy Horse, and Man Afraid. Once gold was discovered in nearby Custer, South Dakota, however, another treaty was signed in 1876 that forced the Sioux onto reservations. Crazy Horse and his tribesmen Gall and Sit-ting Bull refused to go. Their refusal led to Bates' Battle in the Little Big Horn Basin, the Battle of the Rosebud, and eventually to the Battle of Little Big Horn.

Although it only existed for a few short months, Tubb Town sprang up on the Belle Fourche and Custer roads in a way that marked the end of the Sioux era. Ranches opened at the Beaver Stockade and L Open A K, and once

It's hard to tell if anything from the original town still exists at the Tubb Town site, it's so littered with machinery (top) and old lumber (right) from the Accidental Oil Company, the current occupiers of the land. Nearby Newcastle, however, is home to a small museum that preserves a bit of local history.

herders caught wind of the free grazing land, they ran their sheep and set up ranches, too.

A predecessor to modern-day Newcastle, Tubb Town is one of the few ghost towns that was born and died in the same year. Tubb Town's year was 1889. De Loss Tubbs came to the area, built a saloon first and then a building around it, and changed the name from Field City to Tubb Town. He added a store and more bottles to the bar and put in a bed for Calamity Jane, who frequently stopped by. He's also the one who supposedly spread the rumor that the

railroad was planning to pass through. Tubb Town grew to one street, two dance halls, a boardwalk, false-fronted stores, hitching posts, several saloons, and a restaurant. It had a milkman; a Chinese laundry; and whorehouses with names like Big Maude's, the Old Humpy, Jimmie the Tough, Frankie's, and Dippy Dode's.

Families including the Hersham Whites, the McLaughlins, and the Nelsons trickled in. On the day of the Nelsons' arrival, Salt Creek, upon whose east bank Tubb Town rested, flooded and the Nelsons lost everything they owned. Tubbs and Dode, one of the town's many madams, greeted the unfortunate family. Dode insisted that her girls double up and gave the Nelsons a place to sleep. When she realized that they'd also lost their belongings, she sewed clothes and collected money from the other madams for them. The Nelsons accepted the hospitality, but claimed "it is a wretched way to bring up children."

One afternoon during an auction for lumber—a very precious commodity at the time—head madam Frankie outbid everyone assembled for the wood. She had plans, big plans to build "chick sales"—an outhouse—at her establishment because she didn't want to use Tubbs' outhouse in the middle of town anymore. When it came time for the men to build it, Frankie insisted on a one-holer because she had had a two-holer back in Deadwood and her girls had spent too much time talking.

Salt Creek was one-third water, one-third alkali, and one-third epsom salt; it fooled more than one drifter who ended up with stomach pains and diarrhea for weeks. There were many good swimming holes in the area, however, and the whores often swam in the creek naked. Cowboys and children alike often made great sport of stealing the ladies' clothes.

When Calamity Jane visited Tubb Town, she often put on shows. It is also said that Calamity, who was notorious for wearing men's cowboy clothes, once ordered fancy Watteau wrappers—which had back pleats that fell loosely

from neckline to hem—for all the whores in town. She cracked her whip on the counter of Tubbs' General Store, and ordered Fatty the clerk to "git down that bolt of pink china silk. I'll take fifteen yards (13.7 m)." Upstanding, church-going, but much in need of the money, Mrs. Nelson was the Tubb Town seamstress commissioned to do the job. They say she frantically washed and scrubbed her hands after making each one and even disinfected the money she got for the job.

Water was as precious as lumber in Tubb Town. It was Fatty's job to haul water from Beaver Stockade. He loaded, teamed, and unloaded four barrels at a time. On one occasion, a horse backed up into a barrel and relieved himself. Fatty panicked and was afraid he'd lose his job. A bystander who saw the whole thing, however, said "Don't worry, I won't tell on you. What that woman don't know won't hurt her, and besides she won't find it out until she gets to the bottom. By then it'll be too late." Fatty left the water barrel with his customer, didn't say a word about the horse, took the money, and went home.

Judge Stotts set up a printing shop and made eighteen-year-old Frank Nelson his apprentice. The second issue of the *Field City Journal* announced lots for sale in Newcastle two miles (3.2 km) away and Tubb Town shut down. To this day, if anything strange happens in Newcastle, the citizens blame it on the ghost of Tubb Town, known as the Tubb Town "hangover."

The history of Tubb Town (above) is as tied to South Dakota as it is to Wyoming, lying as close to the border as it does. The Black Hills begin only a few miles away, and Mount Rushmore is less than an hour's drive east. To the north, the mining towns of Deadwood and Lead, South Dakota, attract ghost town fans.

Montana

Virginia City

On arriving at this place what astonishes any stranger is the size, appearance, and vast amount of business that is here beheld. Though our city is but a year old, fine and substantial buildings have been erected, and others are rapidly going up. One hundred buildings are being erected each week in Virginia City and environs. . . . Indeed the whole appears to be the work of magic—the vision of a dream. But Virginia City is not a myth, a paper town, but a reality."
—Montana Post, August 27, 1864

It all started in 1863, when Henry Edgar and Bill Fairweather led a group of prospectors through the Yellowstone Valley in search of new diggings. They were repelled by Indians, however, and on May 26 sat dejectedly among the alder bushes on the banks of an unknown creek. As they half-heartedly panned the water, luck was with them, and remarkably they found gold. Soon hundreds and then thousands of prospectors set up camp around the site, scratching and clawing for a piece of the golden pie. Virginia City was to become one of the most lucrative gold camps in the West.

Initially, the miners wanted to name the town that sprouted near the Alder Gulch "Varina" after Jefferson Davis' wife. The judge who recorded the name, however, was from the North. He thought it better to add a few vowels here and a consonant there, and finally changed the name to "Virginia," which ultimately everyone agreed upon. Virginia City officially became an incorporated town—Montana's first—in January 1864. In its first year, $10 million was mined at Alder Gulch, and over the course of its existence, a total of $120 million was extracted. Because of its rapid growth, huge

In 1866, Virginia City (opposite) had already supplanted Bannack as the territorial capital, although many of its buildings were still wood frame with dirt roofs. Restored for tourists, the town today (inset) looks very similar to the town of yesteryear.

Not every building in Virginia City is true to its appearance, however. Some of the structures with old-fashioned signage (opposite) are really motels, gift shops, or modern restaurants. One of the old buildings, set apart from the main drag, houses the local museum, which is a treasure trove for historians. Bank receipts for "clean gold dust" and "trade gold dust" sit within swinging distance from a petrified cat. Gambling wheels, spears used in a Chinese Tong war, arrowheads, and the original Boot Hill headboards just hint at the diversity of the collection.

size, and even bigger gold returns, it replaced Bannack as Montana's second territorial capital one year after its incorporation.

Despite the enormous profits being made in Virginia City—or perhaps because of them—law and order were difficult to maintain. Rules, regulations, politics, and government were completely improvised. Miners' courts were set up with an eye to protecting such things as claims and water rights. There were no prisons in town so any sentences that were handed down were usually clear cut—a transgressor was either hanged, flogged, or exiled, depending on the nature of the crime.

Virginia City's supply of gold dust and nuggets attracted one of the West's most murderous band of thieves. That label alone would have made the story of the Henry Plummer gang memorable, but this far-ranging group of cutthroats was not led by an ordinary outlaw; Henry Plummer, it turned out, was the sheriff of nearby Bannack during his reign of terror. The general consensus was that Plummer stood approximately five foot eight to five foot ten inches (1.73 to 1.78 m) tall and weighed about 150 to 160 pounds (55.95 to 59.68 kg). His chestnut brown hair had flashes of red that set off his steely blue eyes. He was neat and clean, and sported a clipped mustache and a huge slouch hat that he never took off because it hid his strangely shaped head. A favorite with the ladies, Plummer was by all accounts equally charming and magnetic *and* ruthless and murderous.

The gang was organized much like the vigilantes—who later copied the outlaws' setup—with captains, lieutenants, oaths, and secret handshakes. They even had a name: the Innocents, because the gang often used the password, "I am innocent." These unusual road agents were also known to leave a mysterious sign pinned to their victims; it read 3-7-77, and its meaning is still unknown. Plummer never went out himself to commit a crime; he was, instead, a mastermind of organization and planning.

In one incident in August 1863, a man named Lloyd Magruder left Lewiston, Idaho, bound for Virginia City with supplies and gold dust. Along the way, three men from Plummer's gang hired on to Magruder's party. While Magruder slept, the desperados murdered the others, using hatchets and wearing moccasins to put the blame on the Indians; they slaughtered most of the animals, cleaned out the supplies, and took fifty thousand dollars in gold dust. The bandits arrogantly returned to Lewiston where a friend of Magruder's, Hill Beachy, recognized Magruder's riding gear.

Beachy followed the three outlaws' trail across three states before he unraveled the real story and was able to bring the rogues in for their trial and hanging.

But everyone knew the gang's leader was still free and wreaking havoc. Magruder had been popular, and the crime outraged the region. In response, vigilante committees sprang up all over the area. Inspired by a group Hill

Beachy created, Colonel Wilbur Fisk Sanders established a vigilante brotherhood in Virginia City—its structure not unlike Plummer's gang—with a hierarchy and bylaws, a president, an executive officer, a prosecutor, a secretary, a treasurer, and different groups of "soldiers." One time, a vigilante spoke out of turn and revealed details and information about the membership. For his punishment, he was dragged to a cabin, his feet burned, and his fingernails pulled out until he agreed not to talk anymore. The groups had come full circle, from protection to persecution of the public.

The formation of the Virginia City vigilantes threatened other road agents besides Plummer's gang. With the Magruder slaying fresh in their minds, citizens around Alder Gulch were getting fed up. When "Innocent" George Ives killed a slightly retarded German boy who had never hurt a soul, the vigilantes moved to action. They found Ives and promptly hanged him. Although they feared the likes of Boone Helm, a vicious gunman who bragged about eating a man when he was lost in a blizzard in the mountains, they set out to round him up. Helm's final words at the gallows were said to have been, "Three cheers for Jeff Davis!"

The time had come to get the others too, like "Clubfoot" George Lane and Red Yeager. Yeager claimed he wasn't as guilty as his partners, and he quickly revealed the names of everyone in Plummer's gang, including the murderous sheriff. Yeager snitched because,

according to the story, he said, "I don't mind dying, but I'd like to have company."

If the town could've roared, it would've. With Yeager's confession, Colonel Sanders assembled three companies of men to take Plummer and the leader's two deputies, Stinson and Ray. It was dedication to a single purpose that allowed Sanders to succeed. Before long, he had Plummer building the gallows from which he would hang.

With their captain dangling, more of the Innocents were hanged at Virginia City—Jack Gallagher, Frank Parish, and Club-foot Lane. The remaining Plummer bandits—Cyrus Skinner, "Whiskey" Bill Graves, and George Shears, among others—were later rounded up at nearby Hell Gate.

And yet, despite this bloody past and the saloons and dance halls that stayed open all weekend, a great deal of Virginia City's story has little to do with crime. The town took pride in its popular newspaper, the *Montana Post*, and several cultural groups and clubs such as the Keystone Gymnastic Troupe, which billed itself as "a Troupe of Athletes, Dancers, and Negro Minstrels."

Indeed, from all accounts, Virginia City seemed to be a study in contrasts. Honesty and hard work paid off. Fortunes were made over-

night, but not necessarily in the most conventional way. Chinese laundrymen didn't pan the streams, they panned the wash water looking for—and finding—leftover traces of gold. Bartenders grew their fingernails long to catch any extra dust while making a transaction. In these practices and in other ways, Virginia City was much like other booming towns of the West. And its problems were the same, too. Eggs, butter, and flour were scarce (food in general was scarce except for "the same old song"— bread, bacon, beans, and coffee). Yet if a person had the money, he or she could afford fruit, fresh meat, and oysters.

By 1864, Virginia City boomed quickly to a population of nearly ten thousand people. Travelers paid ten dollars a head to pass through the toll gate that led into the settlement. But even as late as 1865, the "city" mainly consisted of a string of log cabins with mud roofs, a couple of stone stores, some frame houses, and the Planter's House, one of the largest of Virginia City's many hotels. It was about three miles (4.8 km) from the east end of Virginia City on one side of Alder Gulch to the west end

Originally known as the New York One Price Clothing Company, the Variety Store (above and right) also displays a bit of historic memorabilia. Close by, the stone building that holds claim to being Montana's oldest Masonic building (c. 1863) is where the vigilantes held court in the basement.

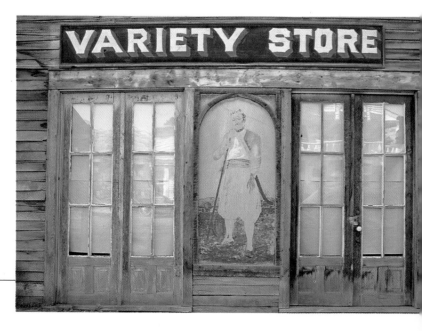

of Nevada City on the other. In the summer, the streets were filled with dust, and in the winter, they were clogged with mud. On the banks of the Gulch, the land was torn up, eaten away by prospector holes and scarred with rubble.

A young man named J. K. Miller passed through Virginia City, staying for a time before he eventually returned East. At seventeen or eighteen years of age, Miller kept a journal of his experiences in Virginia City and the other mining towns he frequented. His account shows a much different picture from the one so often painted of deceit and corruption.

While living in Virginia City, Miller "took the initiatory steps to organize the Virginia City Social Club." He took a sleigh ride that was sponsored by the literary association and attended a society dance. Although he had some lapses from the straight and narrow—he wrote, "*Resolved:* That from this date I do not spend a cent for foolishness such as Billiards, Drinking, Eating, Driving, Riding, Smoking. That I limit my monthly expenses for Dancing and Gifts to ten dollars"—he was often in church and participated in the more civilized, day-to-day aspects of life in town.

Virginia City's population in 1870 had declined to 2,555 "including whites, Chinese and Negroes"; as the gold of Alder Gulch showed signs of petering out, many more made their exodus to other more lucrative sites. Between 1880 and 1900, about 600 people lived there, and by 1940, the population had dwindled to 300. Today, Virginia City ranks among the most popular "restored" ghost towns and receives thousands of visitors each year.

Women, plain and fancy, were also in attendance in town but not at the Masonic lodge. The ladies haberdashery shop (above) catered to the wealthier women in residence.

ENTRANCE TO
HELLGATE CANYON
NEAR HELENA. 1001

Hell Gate and Hell Gate Ronde

It's four long years since I reached this land,
In search of gold among the rocks and sand;
And yet I'm poor when the truth is told.
I'm a lousy miner,
I'm a lousy miner in search of shining gold.

—from the song "Lousy Miner"

In 1860, Frank L. Worden and Captain C. P. Higgins built a log cabin and trading post four miles (6.4 km) west of present-day Missoula and called it Hell Gate Ronde. Carved out by Rattlesnake Creek, which rushes into the Clark Fork of the Columbia River (the locals call it the Missoula River), Hell Gate Canyon stands protected by Mount Jumbo to its north and Mount Sentinel to its south.

By the time Worden and Higgins set up their popular store, however, Hell Gate had long had a forbidding reputation. Fur traders and peaceful tribes who tried to pass westward through the canyon were often ambushed by the hostile Blackfoot Indians. The French called the canyon *Porte de l'enfer*, the Gate of Hell, and the Indians named it *Missoula*, meaning a place of chilling fear.

But in 1862, Lieutenant John Mullan's military trail, Mullan's Road, which stretched 425 miles (683.8 km) from Walla Walla, Washington, made its way through the canyon, and Worden and Higgins were quick to see the business opportunities such a site could offer. During the summer of 1863, hundreds traveled the road from Idaho to the goldfields of Virginia City's Alder Gulch. Higgins, who later donated land to the town of Missoula, and Worden, who later built Missoula's first flour mill, got the supplies for their store in Walla Walla and their produce from the farming regions of the surrounding Bitteroot and Hell Gate valleys.

Montana's first mercantile establishment started out not even as a trading post; it was simply "Worden and Higgins," a small log cabin often used as a chicken coop and surrounded on three sides by pigpens. As more supplies were brought in, a small settlement grew up. Eventually there was a saloon, a trading post, and a smithy. Mullan wrote a travel guide that included Hell Gate. In his book *Mullan's Miners' and Travelers' Guide 1858–62*, he wrote about Worden and Higgins' store: "Road excellent; wood, water, and grass here. Good place to rest animals for a day or two; blacksmith shop at Van Dorn's and supplies of all kinds can be obtained, dry goods, groceries, beef, vegetables and fresh animals if needed." Prices were sky-high. Coffee was eighty cents a pound, sugar sixty cents, and whiskey eight dollars a gallon (and Worden and Higgins made a lot of money selling liquor).

The first marriage of whites in Montana took place at Hell Gate. George White married Mrs. Mineinger in March 1862. According to the story, there wasn't much food to be had for the wedding feast, and so, two men, Frank H. Woody and A. S. Blake, traveled three miles (4.8 km) in the snow to a nearby ranch to see if they could get some chickens. The rancher was away at the time, but had left explicit instructions with the overseer not to sell, lose, or eat any of the chickens. According to Louis Maillet in the Historical Society of Montana's *Contributions*, Blake and Woody "came back the next day with a bag full of chickens. How they got them was never fully known, but it leaked out that Woody talked the man so nearly to death

that the matter became easy." Justice Brooks presided, everyone got drunk, and Blake—who had acted so valiantly about getting the chickens—stole the wedding cake.

Hell Gate was also the site of the first lawsuit ever tried in the state of Montana. Held in Bolt's Saloon, a man called "Tin Cup Joe" accused Baron O'Keefe of killing his horse. According to O'Keefe, the horse kept eating his bales of hay despite O'Keefe's warnings to Joe to keep the horse fenced in. During the opening statements, the judge offended O'Keefe and a fistfight broke out. After the people settled down, the jury reassembled. They voted in favor of Tin Cup Joe, granting him forty dollars in damages, but no one was ever able to collect from O'Keefe.

Montana, they say, had its fair share of rowdy men and lusty women. Perhaps that's why the state has not one, but two Hell Gates: one near Helena (opposite) and the other less than five miles south of Missoula. The community that sprang up within a yodel of Missoula began and ended at the Worden store (below). When Worden and his partner decided to move their establishment to Missoula, Hell Gate died. Ironically, the present city of Missoula long ago burst its former boundaries and now includes the land Hell Gate once sat on.

Although Hell Gate could outfit any miner, frontiersman, or westward-moving wagon for the wilderness or goldfields, a large part of Hell Gate was bad—bad to the bone.

During the winter of 1863–64, members of Henry Plummer's gang used Hell Gate as a headquarters. In 1863, one of the more prominent road agents in Plummer's gang of Innocents, Cyrus Skinner, opened up his Hell Gate Saloon. Skinner's saloon attracted a bad crowd. Road agents George Shears, Bill Hunter, Alex Carter, Whiskey Bill Graves, Johnny Cooper, and Bob Zachary all loitered about Hell Gate and were each suspected of being up to no good. Worden and Higgins had brought a safe— one of the first safes in the region—to their store, which Skinner had a habit of sitting on when he was loafing about. Everyone thought he was going to rob the sixty-five thousand dollars' worth of gold dust Worden and Higgins had locked inside.

These suspicions, combined with the recent confession of Red Yeager in Virginia City and the rounding up of Sheriff Plummer and his deputies, led a posse of twenty-one vigilantes from Alder Gulch to Hell Gate to round up the scoundrels. Skinner, whose prison record showed him to be five nine and a half (1.7 m) with hazel eyes and dark hair, was said to have been deeply respectful of ladies. He had a tattoo of an anchor and a ring on his left hand, a woman and child tattooed on his left arm, and a woman tattooed on his right arm. It was said that he once shot into a campfire thinking he was shooting at Indians, but nearly killed a woman named Mrs. Biddle. Skinner apologized over and over again to the woman and invited her husband, Dr. Biddle, to his saloon for drinks on the house. Mrs. Biddle, who was pregnant at the time, was left to calm her own nerves at the campsite.

When the posse came for Skinner, he stood in the doorway of his Hell Gate Saloon and refused to have his lover, a woman named Nellie, speak on his behalf. During the trial, which was held in Worden and Higgins' store, Skinner sat perched atop the precious safe.

Six members of Plummer's gang, including Skinner, were hanged at Hell Gate. A rope was put around Whiskey Bill Graves' neck as he sat astride a horse. The other end was thrown over the limb of a tree. A vigilante got up on the horse with him and dug his spurs into the horse's side. The vigilante said, "Good-bye, Bill," and Graves was dead. George Shears, one of the more annoying gunmen, was brought to a beam in a barn. When the noose was placed around his neck, he asked, "Should I jump off or slide off?" "Jump," they told him, and he did.

Hell Gate Ronde lasted five years. The first building was put up in Hell Gate in 1860, and during the winter of 1861, the legislature had made Hell Gate the county seat of newly established Missoula County. But by 1865, the town was deserted when Worden and Higgins decided to move their store four miles (6.4 km) away and start up Missoula.

Cinnabar

Thank goodness this blooming town will be wiped off the face of the map when we leave. It's a mystery to me how it got on in the first place.
—Harry Colman, of the Washington Bureau of the Associated Press, *Silver State Post*, June 30, 1938

Cinnabar, with its tiny railway station, fading mines, and humble frontier homes, must not have looked like much to the newsmen, photographers, and officials of the presidential entourage who stopped there for sixteen days in 1903. During late April and early May of that year, Cinnabar acted as a temporary headquarters for President Theodore Roosevelt, who was there to dedicate an arch at nearby Yellowstone Park.

The president's long train of Pullmans and parlor and dining cars chugged into this end-of-the-line town, and through Cinnabar's few telegraph lines, Presidential Secretary William Loeb, Jr., sent messages back and forth to the president and basically conducted affairs of state from the makeshift capital.

Reported to be on land owned by a religious group, Devil's Slide (shown, above, in 1882) is made of the same iron-impregnated rock that caused the Soule brothers to name this spot Cinnabar. To this day, the town site remains clouded. Historians aren't exactly where the town's foundations lie.

Returning to Yellowstone a little more than eleven years after he established the nation's first national park, President Theodore Roosevelt set up office at Cinnabar in 1903. It was the town's finest fortnight.

Cinnabar, located in the southern part of the state along the Montana-Wyoming border, was an unlikely stopover for such high-profile heads of state, especially considering the town's modest and somewhat embarrassing beginnings. Two inexperienced and hapless miners, brothers Charles and James Soule, were the first to believe in the possibilities of the area, although they ultimately left, profitless.

They had been living in a cabin at the southern end of Yellowstone City, making one unsuccessful attempt after another to look for gold and striking only bedrock at Emigrant Gulch. Their dismal record spurred them to set

out on a prospecting trip that took them along the northern boundary of Yellowstone Park. In their travels, they came upon a strange red-colored rock they thought was cinnabar ore. Cinnabar ore contains quicksilver, a scarce product in great demand at the time. They tried hard to keep the secret between them, but the loose-lipped Soule brothers couldn't last out the summer. They went off to Virginia City with samples and announced to anyone who would listen that they'd made an amazing strike and would be happy to stake out claims at one hundred dollars apiece.

Meanwhile, back at Emigrant Gulch, work was stopping because of the terrible freeze of 1865. Returning from their trip to Virginia City, the Soules broadcast to the idle miners at Emigrant Gulch that they'd been asked to stake seven claims for people from Virginia City. As proof, the brothers had with them equipment, supplies, and gunpowder. The rich vein of cinnabar, they said, was just a few miles to the north. Most of the miners at Emigrant Gulch were skeptical, including William McDonnell, an Irish baker, who'd heard them say they would cut a tunnel in the mountain "where the ore is rich, and the quicksilver will seep through the rock and by forming a basin at the bottom of the tunnel, it will collect so that they can dip it out with a cup."

But the Soules were serious and left Gulch to work their newfound lode. They were not skilled miners, however, and ultimately had to ask a more experienced hand, a miner named

Richard Owens, to help them. When Owens took a look at their work, he couldn't believe his eyes. "What are those things that look like rat tails?" he is said to have asked. The rat tails were fuses they told him. The holes were filled with gunpowder, but the fuses they planted had failed to fire off the blast. The Soules were about to dig out the fuses with steel pick-axes when Owens stopped them. Owens admonished them, "Don't you know that if you dig them out with a pick, that steel will strike fire, set off a blast and blow you up?" The Soules had had no idea.

Owens showed them how to wet the tampings and dig out the fuses with a wooden stick. Owens went on to discover some coal outcroppings a couple of miles away from the Soules' mine site, but the brothers failed to see the potential of this discovery. They figured that using coal instead of wood would make it easier for them to extract the quicksilver and were glad that Owens had shown them an easier way. The Soules worked on their tunnel until the spring of 1865 when they finally threw up their hands in disgust and moved on to the more immediate rewards of Helena.

In 1872, famous geologist F. V. Hayden made a geological survey of Montana for the government and traveled to Cinnabar to take rock samples. Hayden discovered that the "red-colored rock" was not cinnabar ore, but iron-impregnated rock. Nevertheless, he named the area Cinnabar in honor of the Soules' "discovery." Hayden also noted the long vertical scars that ran down the face of the mountain and he called this the "Devil's Slide." The story behind the Devil's Slide is captured in an old jingle that has been passed on through the ages:

> Ages ago, one can easily see,
> Old Yellowstone Valley went on a spree;
> The mountains had risen, the valleys had sunk,
> And old Mother Nature got roaringly drunk.
> The Devil, as drunk as the Devil would be,
> Slid to the bottom of Cinnabaree."

Cinnabar, though containing no cinnabar ore, did become the site of the first coal development in the state. The Red Streak Mountain Coal Company, named for the red streaks down the Devil's Slide, was granted a corporate charter in 1864 by the Bannack, Montana, legislature. Cinnabar was chosen by the Northern Pacific as the end of one of its lines and, consequently, became the northern entrance to the fledgling Yellowstone Park in 1883, which is just eight miles (12.8 km) away.

Yellowstone was the nation's first national park, created by an act of Congress in 1872. Most of it lies in Wyoming, but its northern boundary cuts into Montana and its western border into Montana and Idaho. Although Cinnabar served as the railhead for both mining and tourist activity, it died like many other western mining towns. When the Northern Pacific decided to extend its railway to Gardiner's station—still under construction in 1902—Cinnabar faded away.

7. Klondike

Fortymile

The town was almost deserted; men who had been in a chronic state of drunkenness for weeks were pitched into boats as ballast and taken up to stake themselves a claim, and claims were staked by men for their friends who were not in the country at the time.

—surveyor William Ogilvie on Fortymile after Carmack's arrival

In 1867, the United States bought what is now Alaska from the Russians for $7.2 million. Even though it was considered a slight sum for such a large piece of land, some people dubbed the purchase "Seward's Folly." (W. H. Seward, who served as secretary of state from 1861 to 1869, acquired Alaska although public opinion was against him. Few thought Alaska would prove its worth.) Little did they know that within thirty years, a gold rush to rival California's would inundate the territory.

Yet, Alaska and the neighboring Yukon didn't attract prospectors until the 1870s, when the local Indians who held economic sway over the area allowed the newcomers in. By 1880, a man named Edmund Bean and nineteen miners who had given their word to act "as sober, reasonable men" were invited in by a Chilkoot (or Chilkat) chief, Klotz-Kutch. The hearty band led the way for the first prospectors to winter over in the recently acquired land.

Gathering at a store run by a man named McQuesten, the miners began establishing habits and practices that would become the code of the twenty-five hundred or

Two trails took the majority of gold-rushers from the coast of Alaska into Canada: the White Pass and the Chilkoot (opposite, inset). By 1898, when this photograph of the Scales (opposite)—a camp on the Chilkoot trail—was taken, all the paying claims had been taken.

Dyea (below) and Skagway both sit on the northern edge of the Inside Passage in Alaska. Each community had a very distinct personality, in part due to scoundrel Soapy Smith's iron hold over Skagway, which vaunted a mean reputation for lawlessness. Despite this, Skagway was the better rival, for in 1899, the White Pass and Yukon Railroad began service between Skagway and Bennett.

so Klondikers who preceded the rush. One of these rules—the foundation of the Yukon Order of Pioneers—was to tell other prospectors of a strike and to share its wealth. Discoverers received two claims and the others got one, so there was plenty to go around. The placering had up to this point yielded about a million dollars, but that amount was spread among many men, most of whom had camped around Fortymile, which was so named because it lay forty miles (64.3 km) from Fort Reliance, the area's principal trading post where McQuesten first established his store.

The year 1886 produced minor rumblings of success. Franklin Madison worked the Stewart River with his brother, but he said he "did not like the kind of trees that grew on the bars and that gold was never found where wild onions and leeks grew." His quirks prompted him to explore the Fortymile River, where he found coarse gold, enough to put Fortymile on the map and for McQuesten to move his store to

the mouth of the river. Three years later, a saloon opened up, a sign of the steady stream of prospectors who were slowly making their way to the Yukon.

By 1896, twenty Mounties had been posted at the toddler town, an action that was none too soon, for that year marked the discovery that started the new rush. Robert Henderson, a Nova Scotian sailor with a mad drive to find gold, had settled in the area, working tributaries of the Indian River and then crossing to the watershed of the Klondike River. He had plenty of food and kept prospecting and prospecting, finding about two cents per pan.

Henderson was still prospecting when George Washington Carmack and his extended family came upon him. The Tagish Indians, who called the river the Thron-diuck—which led to the word *Klondike*—lived peacefully along the rivers, fishing and hunting. The lifestyle—and the chief's daughter—caught the eye of Carmack, a native Californian and son of a forty-niner. He stayed in the area and eventually married the chief's daughter.

The drive to find gold, however, had not infected Carmack as it had his father, and he searched out Henderson only to trade with him, according to one story; another says he was just out fishing. Whatever his motivation, he came upon Henderson, who was now finding eight cents a pan in a creek he renamed Gold Bottom. Henderson was dreaming of the day "when I got down to bedrock it might be like the streets of the New Jerusalem." He was willing to share the find with Carmack, a white man. But Carmack was traveling with his extended "family": probably his wife, Kate, her brother Skookum Jim Mason (Skookum means "strong" in the Indian dialect), and friend Tagish Charlie. Henderson didn't want the Indians to work the Gold Bottom, so the group left to try a creek about ten miles (16 km) away where earlier they had found a little color. As they left, Henderson asked them to send someone back if they found anything good.

On returning to the spot where they had earlier found gold, the Carmack party panned a few times. That was all they needed to see. Just a little work had produced enough gold dust this time to fill an empty shotgun shell. The fever took hold. Some say Carmack claimed his spots with spruce tree blazes and a hastily written notice on wood, then went to file at Fortymile, the closest Mountie station. Skookum Jim and Tagish Charlie followed suit. It was August.

Typical of the day, although rumor spread that Skookum Jim or Kate had found the

placer site, it was the white man Carmack who got official credit and was allowed to claim the two sites as "discoverer."

It took no time at all for other prospectors to sniff out Bonanza Creek, the new name for the small offshoot of the Klondike, which lay in spruce and white birch country, an area of low hills and plenty of game. Word, however, never reached poor Henderson, who had not even stopped long enough to register his claim with the Mounties. With Carmack's new find, other prospectors came to the area and beat Henderson to the punch. He was left with his one meager claim, although in his old age the Canadian government recognized his contribution and rewarded him with a modest pension.

Meanwhile, the first few doubters in Fortymile had become convinced that Carmack's find was real and good. It was so good for Carmack that he and his relatives later visited Seattle

Since Smith's demise, Dyea has died, but Skagway—the "home of the north winds"—holds its own. Tourism is now its number one industry. Visitors often photograph the more than twenty thousand pieces of local driftwood that form the facade of the Arctic Brotherhood Hall (above).

and booked a stay in the newly opened, imposing Seattle Hotel. Supposedly Kate found the corridors so confusing that she blazed a path from her bedroom door to the front door, cutting away notches in the fine moldings. In a moment of exuberant extravagance, they tossed fifty-cent pieces into the streets from the hotel's roof.

Fortymile itself grew into a bustling center with about ninety cabins and makeshift shacks, six saloons, a dressmaker, a watchmaker, a doctor, two smiths, a library, an opera house where the hurdy-gurdy girls played, and a billiards hall. Fortymile was also becoming known for its forty-rod whiskey. The town's demise, however, was inextricably linked to Carmack's find. Although Carmack had filed his first claim in the crude town, it was not on top of the goldfields and so it passed away, leaving "only the Indians, missionaries, storekeepers, and an honor guard of mounted police," wrote historian Richard Friesen.

Gold dust often accumulated on the floors and tabletops of the bar rooms in the Klondike and all around the west. Clever bartenders grew their fingernails long to gather as much dust as possible in hand. Whoever swept up at night also got extra bonuses if he sifted through the real dust for the gold. It didn't take that much to amass a fortune; this pan holds approximately $35,000 worth of gold.

The Chilkoot Trail

They [the mosquitoes] rise in vast clouds from the peculiar moss along the banks and creeks and their rapaciousness knows no limits. They have been known to drive men to suicide, and the sting of a few dozen will make a man miserable for days. I have seen tough miners sit and cry.

—anonymous chronicler on the trail

In the almost half century since the strike that began the California rush at Sutter's Mill, technological advances had allowed news to travel swiftly—but not in the Klondike. By November 1896, approximately five hundred claims along the renamed Bonanza Creek had been staked out. News had not yet leaked to the "outside," because although news traveled swiftly in the lower forty-eight, it—like the prospectors themselves—had to make the difficult journey to the coast before the trip became easy.

The sourdoughs who wintered in the cold north in 1896–97 and before sought old river beds that hoarded ancient accumulations of gold. In California, the miners dug deep through earth that finally led them to bedrock. In the Klondike, the miners had to contend with the icy, rock-hard permafrost. At first, most of the miners chipped away by day—and in the summer, the days were twenty hours long. But as winter approached and the hours of daylight all but disappeared, one enterprising miner switched the schedule and began working at night, which in the Klondike, allowed him to continue to work a full "day."

To mine in the Klondike, first a fire would be built in an attempt to soften the surrounding permafrost. Then the work went along six inches (15.2 cm) at a time. Miners would leave huge piles of unprocessed, dug-up permafrost until spring when the water was flowing again and could wash through and separate the gold from the waste. The soon-to-be millionaires would dig side by side with others destined to paupers. Occasional tests kept the miners on track, but it didn't tell them the full story of their success or failure. They all had to wait for the thaw.

The wintertime also brought incredible, mind-boggling cold. Without thermometers, the men improvised, using whatever liquids were on hand. They put out bowls of liquid, and depending on when they froze, they'd know the temperature. The freezing points of each liquid gave them an indication of whether it was safe to go outside or not. Mercury froze at $-38°F$ ($-39°C$); whiskey at $-55°F$ ($-48°C$); and kerosene at $-65°F$ ($-54°C$). The only other fluid on hand that froze at a colder temperature was Perry Davis' Pain Killer, which solidified at a whopping $-75°F$ ($-59°C$), a temperature that shut in even the most determined adventurer.

Even when the weather warmed up to less bone-chilling extremes, the cold penetrated the miners' simple moss-chinked cabins.

Weather entered the cramped quarters in the form of icicle-like "glaciers," or thin crusts, thanks to the moisture-laden cooking steam. When the stoves heated up, the frozen ceiling ice rained down on the men for hours. Nothing remained dry. The only advantage, perhaps, was that the icicles saved the men from going outside to get ice for melting down. But heat was a serious affair. A Klondiker couldn't be lazy. Everything turned brittle in the cold. If the stove wasn't fired up, the axe, which out of necessity had to be stored nearby, could crack. If the metal cracked, a miner couldn't cut more wood. And without more wood, he'd most surely die.

These men were hardened; most had worked other goldfields and they knew how easily life parted from the unwary or the inept. When they were able to leave when the spring thaw came, they hopped the few steamboats that ran to accommodate the fur traders. From St. Michaels, they booked passage on the *Excelsior* to San Francisco and on the *Portland* to Seattle. The news preceded them. Crowds flocked to the docks to watch the grizzled men disembark. Some carried the gold in suitcases (one was so heavily laden that the handles broke off), pickle jars, and "pokes," which were sacks made out of caribou or moose hide. One grapefruit-size poke might weigh one hundred pounds (37.3 kg).

In summer, the sun shines almost twenty-four hours a day in Dawson. Its extreme location hindered thousands from reaching their goal, yet by 1898 (above) thousands did make it, only to find barely livable conditions and already claimed stakes. By June, the town's population was bursting at 28,000. To help them through their stay, 120,000 gallons of whiskey were supposedly shipped in that year.

For many years before the discovery of gold in the Klondike, the powerful Chilkoot tribe controlled the pass. Because no glaciers crossed the passageway through the mountains, it became one of the most important corridors in the territory. Once the Chilkoots opened the trail to foreigners, they continued to hold a monopoly on carrying goods over the pass for a fee. On the average, a Chilkoot man (below) could carry 150 pounds (78 kg) a day. The "Golden Stairs" (opposite, top) were so steep and narrow that stampeders had to take them in single file. The two men who carved the steps exacted a toll from every person for every trip up. People packed kittens, pianos, even steamboats over the pass. A monument to the Klondike Pioneers (opposite, bottom) was erected in Dawson.

The banner headlines screamed the news. The Seattle *Post-Intelligencer* ran:

GOLD! GOLD! GOLD!
Sixty-Eight Rich Men on
The Steamer *Portland*
STACKS OF YELLOW METAL.

And at what turned out to be a disservice to most, the dispatches hastened across the country, sparking more and more people to put down their work and take up the dream. Want ads appeared everywhere. It was said that unpicked fruit ripened on the trees in the California valleys, jurors jumped from their boxes before delivering a verdict, and tailors, teachers, and even nuns joined in the rush to book passage however they could to get up north.

Guidebooks recommended all sorts of things—some useful, some downright stupid. They told travelers to bring sled dogs and pack horses; so the newcomers brought animals all right, but most were untrained and utterly useless. Seattle residents, story goes, had to lock up their dogs for fear the miners would spirit them away overnight.

Some folks traveled over land, others by slow boat to St. Michaels to reach the Klondike. Most, however, got to Dyea or Skagway and began their real trek from there.

The rush to the Yukon was unlike any other. More than one hundred thousand people supposedly left homes and jobs to seek their fortune in a harsh territory they knew nothing about; by the time the majority got there, all claims were taken. Some had endured life-threatening avalanches, snowblindness, tempest-tossed rapids, and starvation for nothing. The disappointment and defeat was practically tangible; many died. Others, however, claimed it was by far the best experience of their lives.

The newcomers were called "cheechakos," as opposed to the sourdoughs who'd stayed at least one winter and nourished themselves with bread made from a sourdough yeast. These cheechakos might choose to go by boat to St. Michaels and then on eastward to Dawson, but the boat was slow and crowded, the route was longer (about 1,700 miles [2735.3 km]), and the Yukon River froze more months of the year than it ran. The shorter routes ran to Dawson from Skagway over the White Pass and from Dyea over the Chilkoot Pass. The trailheads for the White and the Chilkoot passes were only six miles (9.6 km) apart. Yet each path had a very distinct personality.

Although not a ghost town, at its peak the Chilkoot had a number of small camps and "towns" along its path, including Sheeps or Sheep Camp at timberline and the Scales at the foot of the summit. For that reason, the trail is included here. Today, the Chilkoot Trail is part of the Klondike Gold Rush Park.

Generally, if a prospector had horses or pack dogs, he'd take the forty-five-mile (72.4 km) Skagway Trail over the White Pass, which was longer but less steep than the thirty-mile (48.2 km) Chilkoot or Dyea Trail. The Chilkoot Trail ran over a pass that was 3,550 feet (1,082 m) high. Knee deep in mud and lousy with rocks and dead horses in summer and covered with rotten ice in winter, the trail to the foot of the summit was just a hint of what was to come. The final half mile (.81 km) alone was an intimidating one thousand feet (304.8 m) straight up. The men and the few women who climbed this last leg of the pass up the steep mountainside were forced to walk in single file, leaning forward. Men dressed sensibly, but the hundred or so women who crossed the pass usually wore corsets, tight-fitting jackets, and long skirts rather than the layered clothing more practical for the extremes of exertion-induced sweats and chilling winds.

An average white man carried fifty pounds (18.6 kg) on his back; an average Chilkoot man could carry one hundred and fifty pounds (55.9 kg). Most white women did not carry packs, but the Chilkoot women might tote seventy-five pounds (27.9 kg), and their children, upwards of thirty pounds (11.1 kg). The Chilkoot established a monopoly on the mountainside, which many cheechakos took advantage of.

The rushers brought with them one to two thousand pounds (373 to 746 kg) of goods and food per person, at first because it made sense but later because the Royal Canadian Mounted Police insisted on it. Too many travelers were passing from Alaska into Canada with unrealis-

tic expectations—little money, less food, and much hope. The first wave of prospectors almost starved in Dawson one winter and the Mounties did not want a repeat occurrence, so they established a station at the top of the path to check each person's stock of food, which was supposed to equal half a year's supply.

Those who couldn't or wouldn't carry their own goods needed about four hundred dollars for the packing fees, a whopping sum considering that the supplies themselves probably cost only three hundred dollars. Many people turned back. Whoever bore the burden of the goods still had to deal with the weather, and no matter how skilled the packer, it took about thirty-five to forty trips, or three months, to

Supply List From 1897

GROCERIES

400 lbs. (149.2 kg) Flour
50 lbs. (18.6 kg) Rice
25 lbs. (9.3 kg) Rolled oats
50 lbs. (18.6 kg) Sugar
150 lbs. (55.9 kg) Bacon
25 lbs. (9.3 kg) Dry salt pork
100 lbs. (37.3 kg) Beans
15 lbs. (5.6 kg) Salt
75 lbs. (27.9 kg) Dried fruits
20 lbs. (7.4 kg) Coffee
10 lbs. (3.7 kg) Tea
25 lbs. (9.3 kg) Evaporated potatoes
5 lbs. (1.8 kg) Evaporated onions
25 lbs. (9.3 kg) Dried beef
8 lbs. (2.9 kg) Baking powder
1 Commissary box

3 pkgs. Yeast cakes
6 2-oz. (62.1 g) Jars beef extract
5 lbs. (1.8 kg) Evaporated soup vegetables
1 qt. (.946 l) Bottle evaporated vinegar
1 pt. (.473 l) Ginger
5 lbs. (1.8 kg) Butter
1 lb. (373 g) Pepper
1 lb. (373 g) Mustard
½ lb. (186.5 g) Each, cinnamon, allspice, and ginger
20 lbs. (7.4 kg) Candles
2 doz. cans Cond. milk
1 tin Matches
5 lbs. (1.8 kg) Laundry soap
5 lbs. (1.8 kg) Toilet soap
3 lbs. (1.1 kg) Soda

CLOTHING

1 Suit Mackinaw
1 Suit heavy canvas
1 Heavy wool overshirt
2 Lighter wool overshirts
1 Suit oil skins
2 Suits heavy wool underwear
2 Suits light underwear, mixed
1 Large silk muffler
1 pr. 10 to 14 lb. (3.7 to 5.2 kg) blankets
1 pr. 8 to 10 lb. (2.9 to 3.7 kg) blankets
1 Broad-brimmed hat
1 Sweater

4 prs. Woolen mits
1 pr. Oil gloves
1 pr. Rubber gloves
1 pr. High-top leather boots
1 pr. Best heavy shoes
1 pr. Best rubber boots
1 pr. Felt boots
1 pr. Arctic shoes
1 doz. pr. Socks, mixed
2 pr. German socks
1 Sleeping bag
4 Towels
3 yds. (2.7 m) Mosquito net

Two pieces waterproof canvas, 6 by 10 feet (1.8 by 3 m), to cover goods.
Extra lacings for boots, and shoemaker's thread, needles, wax, and nails, for repairing.
Pins, safety pins, needles, thread.

HARDWARE, TOOLS, ETC.

1 Yukon sled
1 pr. Snowshoes
1 Yukon stove, heavy steel
2 Fry pans
1 Gold pan
1 Nest granite buckets
3 Granite plates
2 Granite cups
1 Dish pan (retinned)
1 Milk pan (retinned)
2 sets Knives and forks
2 Spoons
1 Basting spoon
1 Coffeepot
1 Butcher knife
1 Can opener
1 Pocketknife
1 Hunter's knife
1 Whetstone
1 pr. Shears
1 Miner's candlestick
1 Emery stone
1 Axe, single bit
1 Pick
1 Shovel, spring point
1 Broad hatchet, or hunter's axe
1 Claw hammer
1 Brace and 3 bits (¼, ½, ⅞-in.) (.61, 1.27, 2.22 cm)
1 Whipsaw with handles
1 Handsaw

1 Wooden Jack plane
1 Extra axe handle
6 Handsaw files
6 8-in. (20.3-cm) Mill files
6 10-in. (25.4-cm) Mill files
1 2-ft. (60.9-cm) Rule
1 Padlock
1 Tape line
1 Chalk line
5 Cakes blue chalk
1 Compass
1 Spool copper wire
1 Spring balance
25 lbs. (9.3 kg) Nails, assorted
1 pr. Gold scales
1 Money belt
2 Buck pouches
2 Hasps and staples
2 prs. Strap hinges
5 lbs. (1.8 kg) Pitch
3 lbs. (1.12 kg) Oakum
3 balls Candle wick
5 lbs. (1.8 kg) Quicksilver
1 Pack strap
150 ft. (45.7 m) ½ in. (1.2 cm) Manilla rope
4 pkgs. Hob nails
1 Draw knife
3 Chisels, (½, ⅞ and 1-in.) (1.27, 2.22, 2.54 cm)
1 Rip saw
1 One-man saw

FIREARMS

1 Rifle, 30-30 Winchester
Fishing tackle
1 Single-barrel shotgun
Ammunition

DRUGS

Portable medicine chest, containing medicines and drugs.

transfer a full outfit across the pass even though each trip itself only took a day.

Once over the pass, the cheechakos dumped their belongings in a pile, marked them, and if the snow was right, sledded down through shoulder-high ruts back to the Scales, the stopping-off camp just before the steepest climb. It was here that everyone reassessed their loads, for it was also here that the packers raised their prices per pound. Much was left by the side of the path, and enterprising men collected and resold articles to newcomers fresh off the boats in Dyea or Skagway. Before a tram was built in later years to carry people over the pass, at least twenty thousand "rushers" had pushed themselves over the mountainous barrier to their dreams.

The Chilkoot Trail, like the Skagway Trail, led into Lake Bennet, where the trekkers proceeded to build boats that would take them the approximately five hundred miles (804.5 km) remaining over water to Dawson. It took most Klondikers the whole summer of 1897 to cross over into Canada with their supplies. They spent the autumn building the boats and then waited for the spring thaw before setting out for Dawson. In 1898, the ice cracked on May 29, mobilizing some seven thousand handmade and not altogether riverworthy boats.

That summer of 1897—when the most people crossed the pass—is recorded in a number of diaries and letters.

Arizona Charley Meadows, a former star of Buffalo Bill's Wild West Show, and his wife Mae McKamish Meadows—also a talented rider and sometime entertainer—packed up to go. In a letter posted from Juneau, she wrote:

We read a letter here from a woman in Dawson, and I tell you it would make you want to have a flying machine and go at once. The people have gold sacked up like wheat lying all around. If we can only get in, we will be ready to come back next summer and buy out Santa Cruz.

They reached Sheep Camp, a stopping-off place, in September 1897 with a portable general store and bar and set about selling drinks to other travelers. Mae was in camp on September 18, the day that they were going to move to the foot of the summit. That day was a memorable one. As she tells it:

The river came up into the big tent about two o'clock in the night. Charlie and I were sleeping on the ground in the corner, and we woke up to find a foot (30.4 cm) of water in the tent—up to our first blanket—and the wind blowing a perfect gale.

Charley wisely moved Mae to the highest, driest place there was—on top of the saloon bar—because less than five hours later, a landslide churned up a wall of black dust, dirty snow, and falling trees. Moments later a flood came roaring toward Sheep Camp. Charley rushed in to warn Mae and to hurry her up the slope and away from danger. Not a minute too soon. The slide destroyed their tent and sent Mae's last trunk (their other belongings had al-

Unlike many of the miners, the indigenous Indian tribes in the north (above) had adapted to their surroundings. Food may not always have been plentiful, but with skill, hunters often provided more than enough meat to get them and their families through the tough winters.

ready been moved up the trail) spinning its way down "to Frisco."

It was terrible. Charley said if he had a Kodac [sic] of me as I was running from the Sheeps Camp flood, there would not be any use of going to the Klondike as that would be a gold mine itself. . . . You could not see the people for the mud going back to God's country. People could not get out fast enough.

But Mae and Charley were not discouraged. With a little searching, they found the big tent and Mae replaced her missing underclothes by buying some from a woman heading back to San Francisco. They then encountered their last great obstacle: the pass itself.

The year 1898 was a warm one in the Yukon. It warmed the hearts of Marie Isharov, a twenty-year-old Polish native, and Frank Brady, a Montana miner ten years her senior. They met on the trail, and as they picked their way through the unknown landscape, they fell in love. In early April, a minister from Missouri married them at the top of the pass while onlookers—"many of them with loads of one hundred pounds (37.3 kg) on their backs," wrote an eyewitness—cheered from below. Thanks to one of the groom's friends, the cere-

mony even benefited from accordion music, including Lohengrin's "Wedding March." And the ring was made from nugget gold found by another of the groom's buddies.

But the warm weather brought tragedy as well. Just one week later, still in snow season, the comparatively balmy daytime temperatures loosened the winter's icy accumulations. Snow fell—from the sky but also from the mountain. Despite the Indians' attempts to warn people away from the trail, a great landslide crashed down the mountain about two miles (3.2 km) from Sheep Camp, burying approximately forty men.

According to one account, travelers rushed to help, digging out survivors and those less fortunate. When one woman was dug up, she immediately directed the workers to where her husband lay trapped under the snow. As soon as they succeeded uncovering him, a voice boomed that another avalanche was on its way. Everyone ran for their lives, and the poor man who had just been saved was buried alive once more. The rescuers failed to find him a second time.

Other odd stories surfaced. The slide was so sudden and had so much force that it cleaved its way down the mountain, cutting its

path sharply, so sharply, in fact, that it cut one tent in two, leaving one camper sleeping soundly while the other was carried away to his death.

The survivors attempted to bury the dead with dignity. They used precious wood for makeshift coffins and black cloth for the lining. If anyone knew the deceased's name or history, it was written up, sealed in a bottle, and placed in the coffin before burial.

No one knows how many people died on the pass and on the trails leading up to it, but death was not uncommon. The luckiest ones got to Dawson and made their fortunes; others were lucky enough to turn back and make it home with their health intact. Of the one hundred thousand or so who attempted the route to Dawson, only thirty or forty thousand ever reached Dawson. Of the few hundred who got rich, only a handful kept their fortunes. Historians estimate that the Klondikers spent from thirty to sixty million dollars to reach Dawson; in comparison, the mines barely produced ten million dollars the peak year of the rush.

Women made their way to the Klondike on their own and with their partners. These women (below) in Dawson took time out from their "drinking bee" to pose for a photograph.

Fortymile Forty-rod

To make the whiskey that the Fortymilers favored, just follow the directions below. (Actually, don't try it; just appreciate the art of the recipe!)

Take of sugar or molasses an unlimited quantity; add a small percentage of dried fruit or, in summer, berries; with sour dough, flavor to taste with anything handy—the higher flavored the better— such as old boots, discarded (and unwashed) foot rags, and other delicacies of a similar nature. After fermentation, place in a rough sort of still, for preference an empty kerosene tin, and serve hot according to taste.

A DRINKING BEE AT WHITE CHAPEL, DAWSON.

den by the Mounties to cross the White Horse Rapids, a particularly dangerous portion of the Yukon River, and many resorted to disguise to get across. More than one woman crossed the high passes without a male escort and more than one probably donned Klondike gear and wore her hat low on her head as she piloted a boat across the raging water.

One of the most interesting success stories is that of Belinda Mulrooney, who arrived in the Dawson area in the spring of 1897 with silk and cotton cloth and hot water bottles, items of luxury she figured few people would have brought in and many would want. She figured right and made a reported 600-percent profit that immediately went into new investments including a restaurant and houses. "There was nowhere then in Dawson for the newcomers to live and lumber was as scarce as hens' teeth," she said. She bought up as many small boats as she could, broke them down for their boards, and built shelters. Not a bad idea: she was providing a public service *and* making quite a healthy profit.

With a growing nest egg, Mulrooney turned her sights to the goldfields themselves. Within a mile and a half (2.4 km) of Carmack's original claim on Bonanza Creek, Mulrooney established a hotel and another restaurant. Her knack for hotels peaked in Dawson, though, when she built the grand Fair View Hotel overlooking the river. She was in her mid-twenties when she brought Dawson its first real elegance in the form of cut-glass chandeliers,

With money came hardship. Conditions were far below standard in Dawson (above), but it did not daunt the resourceful. While some men threw their shirts away for lack of laundry soap, others salvaged them, cleaned them as best they could and resold them, sometimes to their original owners.

Dawson

There is always a crowd of men waiting outside the recorder's office. I waited from Monday to 3 P.M. Friday before my turn came. Finding that there was apparently not the slightest chance to get anything I decided to return home.
—anonymous Klondiker

Throughout the West, women made their way to gold camps as dance-hall girls and prostitutes, but they also came as dentists, doctors, surveyors, and businesspeople, finding that the men were often less biased once the initial barriers were broken down. Although the Klondike attracted many women, they were forbid-

damask linens, china, silverware, Belgian carpets, lace curtains, and brass bed frames. The thirty-room hotel that charged $11.50 a day for lodging and food eventually had paned-glass windows, telephones, hot-air heating, and electric lights, comforts practically unimaginable at that time in that place.

But it took a while to put it all together. Her packer quit her service before he brought anything over the passes, although he kept her four-thousand-dollar advance. One shipment of chairs got through, but the chair legs had been left behind on the docks at St. Michaels. She was clever, however, took problems in stride, and amassed a great fortune. It didn't hurt that over the course of her stay in the Yukon she overheard many miners talking, and that talk often led to investments which led to even more money. But that didn't cause her to ease up, for she also had a hand in starting up the telephone and water companies.

Her history beyond Dawson shows her extraordinary gumption. After marrying a man who claimed to be a baron and who squandered her fortune in Europe, Mulrooney returned to the North, not to Dawson but to work her magic in the Fairbanks gold rush.

As Mulrooney was establishing herself, another woman made her way to Dawson: Nettie Hoven. Hoven braved the way from New York City to Dawson in seven months. She and her lover, John Mellen, signed up to work on a ship bringing Mrs. Hannah Gould and 150 widows to the Klondike. In Rio de Janeiro, the ship broke down. Running through the treacherous Strait of Magellan, they crashed into rocks. By the time they reached Valparaiso, the women realized the ship's company had no funds to get them safely to their destination. Not settling for defeat, the undaunted band raised enough money to continue to Seattle.

Nearly all had paid in advance for outfits which were to be ready for them at Seattle together with a steamer to convey them to Dawson. Outfits and steamer alike failed to materialize, and as a result nearly all my fellow passengers on the Columbia are still stranded in Seattle.

For the plucky Miss Hoven, the problems in Seattle gave her just the chance she needed. Mellen had threatened to kill her, and she gave him the slip by stowing away on the *Hayden Brown*. It was a simple act. She walked aboard just as the boat was about to pull away from the dock. No one questioned her until it was too late to turn back. She was treated well and even given some work to do in exchange for her passage.

On landing at St. Michaels, Nettie still needed to secure passage to Dawson. All the boat captains refused to let her work her way to the Klondike boomtown, except one. Upon hearing her story, Captain Danaher welcomed her aboard with all the privileges of a paying passenger.

Nettie's is a Cinderella story. Although Mellen followed her to Dawson, she went to the courts for protection, which they granted.

Mellen stayed away and Miss Hoven happily became Mrs. Fred Thoerner in August 1898.

Dawson had its fair share of fortunate men as well—one in particular who no one thought would ever make it with even a modicum of success. "The Lucky Swede" Anderson paid $800 for a mine that everyone took to be worthless. Not too long after, the lucky man had taken $1,200,000 from within its boundaries.

"Big" Alex McDonald was another man of great flamboyance who loved his mines. His Thirty-Six Mine consistently yielded sensational nuggets in great quantities. It was said that he stashed his nuggets in a bowl in his dining room. "Help yourself. Take some of the bigger ones," he told a newspaper reporter who interviewed him. She hesitated but Alex waved her on. "Take as many as you please. There are lots more." The biggest chunk to have come from the mine—and probably from the Klondike itself—weighed in at three and a half pounds (1.3 kg). It was valued at about six hundred dollars.

Tall tales circulated with great ease, but one man reportedly panned sixty-one thousand dollars in one day, although an eight-hundred-dollar daily take was considered well above expectations. The wealth trickled down, so even those not involved in mining reaped great rewards. As to be expected, businesspeople benefited, but so did bartenders who, like their counterparts in the Rockies, grew their fingernails long in an attempt to scrape up a little extra gold dust. Whoever swept up the bars also took in an added bonus, sometimes almost as much as one hundred dollars from the gold dust mixed into the sawdust.

With so much visible success, it might have been hard to imagine Dawson's first winter during the rush when cheechakos flocked to the city thinking they'd find plenty of food and supplies. That winter of 1897 courted disaster. As newcomers traveling east arrived from St. Michaels, more were coming from the Chilkoot and White Passes in the south, while others were leaving Dawson traveling west with the news that food was scarce. And scarce it was. The Mounties had counted on ships coming through with food, but these were being waylaid at some of the gold camps closer to St. Michaels.

The changing patterns of temperature and ice buildup also proved hazardous. Two boats, each carrying one thousand pounds (373 kg) of food, succumbed to the unpredictable ice, while the crew of another boat voluntarily ditched its load to save the ship, also from ice. Yet another boat that was supposed to have food in its hold came with whiskey and furniture instead. Even the caribou were not to be found that winter. The Mounties managed to scrounge supplies from neighboring posts and Indian tribes, enough to save the citizens of Dawson, but the Indians suffered that winter, too, and many of them died.

Dawson was named for George Mercer Dawson, chief of the Geological Survey of Canada. From its humble beginnings in a few canvas

WATSON BLOCK, DAWSON Y.T. SEPT '99,

tents, the town boomed quickly and brightly. By the summer of 1897, the town's three hundred buildings included ten saloons that were making upward of two thousand dollars each week. A year later, with the population at an all-time high of about twenty-eight to thirty thousand, a corner lot on Front Street, the town's main street, went for approximately forty thousand dollars. Lemons sold for one dollar apiece, tomatoes five dollars a pound, watermelons were twenty-five dollars, and a broom brought in fifteen dollars.

The city was a modern marvel, equipped with telephones, electricity, and even moving pictures. Yet these conveniences still couldn't turn a frontier town into anything but what it was. The streets were still muddy paths flanked by wooden boardwalks, and many citizens still lived in hastily thrown together shanties and canvas-and-board shacks. The frontier mentality made for interesting details. During a crucial moment in the Spanish-American

War, a newspaper was auctioned off for fifty dollars. The buyer turned around and made one thousand dollars by renting a hall and charging one-dollar admission to all who wanted to hear the news read aloud. Even the bank did not escape that certain mix of eagerness and bravado: It was not uncommon for huge sums in gold to be kept unguarded in wooden boxes.

Dawson lived through three fires and was rebuilt each time. Disaster didn't stop its forward motion. It was the common disease of western mining towns that crippled Dawson: word of another supposedly bigger and better strike. This time the gold was in Nome, and Dawson lost most of its population. Dawson never quite died, though. In 1966, the last gold-dredge operation shut down, but tourism has carried the town's approximately 700 residents through the years. The public's healthy curiosity for former boomtowns has even recently boosted the population. As of 1989, Dawson's census totaled 1,698 residents.

In 1899, Dawson (left) was still at its peak. The Northwest Mounted Police had sway over the people and order reigned. Saloons and stores closed on Sundays and cutting wood was prohibited, but dancing, gambling, and attending the theater were allowed. Seven theaters, three of which were in tents, played to a population of about thirty thousand. The price of admission included a drink or a cigar. Writers followed the actors. Well after the gold rush ended, poet Robert Service made his way to the Klondike, first to Whitehorse, then to Dawson, where he composed "Ballads of a Cheechako" in 1909. He then wrote his first novel, using wallpaper and wrapping paper, which at that time were cheaper than stationery.

REFERENCES AND FURTHER READING

Aikman, Duncan. *Calamity Jane and the Lady Wildcats*. Lincoln, Nebraska: University of Nebraska, 1927.

Anonymous. *The Banditti of the Rocky Mountains*. Notes and bibliography by Jerome Peltier. Minneapolis: Ross & Haines, Inc., 1964.

Ashbaugh, Don. *Nevada's Turbulent Yesterday . . . A Study in Ghost Towns*. Los Angeles: Westernlore Press, 1980.

Botkin, B. A.,ed. *A Treasury of American Folklore: Stories, Ballads and Traditions of the People*. New York: Crown Publishers, 1948.

Brown, Robert L. *Jeep Trails to Colorado Ghost Towns*. Caldwell, Idaho: The Caxton Printers, Ltd., 1963.

Clark, Thomas D. *Gold Rush Diary: Being the Journal of Elisha Douglass Perkins on the Overland Trail in the Spring and Summer of 1849*. Lexington: University of Kentucky Press, 1967.

Corle, Edwin. *Death Valley and the Creek Called Furnace*. Los Angeles: The Ward Ritchie Press, 1962.

Davis, Jean. *Shallow Diggin's: Tales from Montana's Ghost Towns*. Caldwell, Idaho: The Caxton Printers, Ltd., 1962.

Eberhart, Perry. *Guide to the Colorado Ghost Towns and Mining Camps*. Denver, Colorado: Sage Books, 1959.

Florin, Lambert. *Western Ghost Towns*. Seattle: Superior Publishing Co., 1961.

Hunt, Inez. *Ghost Trails to Ghost Towns*. Denver, Colorado: Sage Books, 1958.

Jenkinson, Michael. *Ghost Towns of New Mexico: Playthings of the Wind*. The University of New Mexico Press, 1967.

Kirk, Ruth. *Exploring Death Valley* (third edition). Stanford: Stanford University Press, revised 1981.

Koenig, George. *"23" Skidoo and Panamint, Too!*, Keepsake no. 11. Death Valley: 22nd Death Valley '49ers Encampment, 1971.

Kunze, C. E. and C. B. Glasscock. *The Death Valley Chuckwalla*, vol. 1, no. 3, February 15, 1907.

Lingenfelter, Richard E. *Death Valley & the Amargosa: A Land of Illusion*. Berkeley: University of California Press, 1986.

Looney, Ralph. *Haunted Highways: The Ghost Towns of New Mexico*. New York: Hastings House, Publishers, 1968.

Lucia, Ellis. *Tough Men, Tough Country*. Englewood Cliffs, NJ: Prentice-Hall, 1963.

Mather, R. E. and F. E. Boswell. *Hanging the Sheriff: A Biography of Henry Plummer*. Salt Lake City, Utah: University of Utah Press, 1987.

Mazzulla, Fred and Jo. *Al Packer: A Colorado Cannibal*. Denver, Colorado: Fred and Jo Mazzula, 1968.

McDonald, Douglas. *Nevada Lost Mines & Buried Treasures*. Las Vegas: Nevada Publications, 1981.

McGrath, Roger D. *Gunfighters, Highwaymen & Vigilantes: Violence on the Frontier*. Berkeley: University of California Press, 1984.

McNeer, May. *The Alaska Gold Rush*. New York: Random House, 1960.

Paher, Stanley W. *Death Valley Ghost Towns*. Las Vegas: Nevada Publications.

Pence, Mary Lou, and Lola M. Honsher. *The Ghost Towns of Wyoming*. New York: Hastings House, Publishers, 1956.

Pierce, Philip. *Ghost Town Directory of the West*. Cheyenne, Wyoming: Pierce Publishing Co., 1964.

Rolle, Andrew, ed. *The Road to Virginia City: The Diary of James Knox Polk Miller*. Norman, Oklahoma: University of Oklahoma Press, 1960.

Sagan, Robert. "A Little Timberland 'Tomflumery,'" *American West*, November/December 1985.

Silverberg, Robert. *Ghost Towns of the American West*. New York: Thomas Y. Crowell Company, 1968.

Toole, K. Ross. *Montana: An Uncommon Land*. Norman, Oklahoma: University of Oklahoma Press, 1959.

Urbanek, Mary. *Place Names of Wyoming*.

U.S. Works Progress Administration. *Wyoming: A Guide to Its History, Highways, and People*. New York: Oxford University Press, 1941.

U.S. Works Progress Administration. *Colorado: A Guide to the Highest State*. New York: Hastings House, Publishers, 1941.

U.S. Works Progress Administration. *Montana: A State Guide Book*. New York: Viking Press, 1939.

Varney, Philip. *New Mexico's Best Ghost Towns*. Flagstaff, Arizona: 1981.

Wallace, Robert. *The Miners*. New York: Time-Life Books, 1976.

Wolle, Muriel Sibell. *The Bonanza Trail: Ghost Towns and Mining Camps of the West*. Bloomington: Indiana University Press, 1955.

Wolle, Muriel Sibell. *Montana Pay Dirt: A Guide to the Mining Camps of the Treasure State*. Denver, Colorado: Sage Books, 1963.

Index